PRESENTED TO:

_____

FROM:

_____

DATE:

_____

LIVE LEARN LEAD

TO MAKE A DIFFERENCE

by

DON SODERQUIST

Copyright © 2006, 2014 by Don Soderquist
Published by The Soderquist Center,
2000 West University Street
Siloam Springs, Arkansas 72761
www.soderquist.org

Contributing Writer: Mark Gilroy | www.markgilroy.com

ISBN 978-0-9911067-0-7

Printed in the United States of America

TABLE OF CONTENTS

PREFACE
LIVE, LEARN, LEAD

I enjoy life! For me, life is a great adventure. I thank God for each new day and look forward to the opportunities that He has in store for me. The journey for each of us is special and unique.

Live, Learn, Lead was first published in 2006. It was a way for me to share my deeply held beliefs with others who might be facing or getting ready to face some of the same experiences I have had as a Christian, business leader, a husband, and a father. As I picked up the book and read through it again, I was amazed by how much has happened in our world in a few short years.

The biggest example is that in 2006 we hadn't experienced the dramatic unraveling of so many basic elements of our economy and way of life that occurred with the jarring global financial collapse of 2007 – 2008. That brought a lot of baggage with it, from high unemployment and underemployment rates to significant damage to home values and the overall real estate market, to a ballooning national debt crisis, not just for the United States, but for many countries. So much rises and falls on leadership. I still wonder if we would have had to experience all that turmoil if the leaders—and really all individuals—within our society were more committed to living, learning, and leading with the highest of values and convictions.

Knowing how much we have gone through led me to review the content, freshen up the material, and bring the message up to date.

This edition has updates and revisions throughout. But, in rereading *Live, Learn, Lead*, I was delighted to find that the principles I wrote about in 2006 still apply today. In my mind, the basic principles have not changed at all. In fact, they are more relevant in the world we live in today—and I recognize fully that some of you face tougher business conditions than I did during my career at Walmart—than when I first wrote the book.

As I read words that were written almost ten years ago, I was reminded that there are timeless principles that are fundamental to the orderly functioning of a civilized society. These principles of life are trans-generational and apply where and whenever we live. I believe that when we hold fast to these foundational principles as a nation, as organizations, as families, and as individuals, we can avoid the deep traumas we have experienced in recent years. Oh sure, there is an economic cycle. There are ups and downs in life. But much of what we have experienced is a consequence of active violation of the values and principles that have brought so much blessing and prosperity to us.

As you read this revised and updated edition of *Live, Learn, Lead*, consider the timeliness and timelessness of these principles. Notice that they go beyond the workplace as well.

I am more committed than ever to letting these truths continue to be those that guide the way I try to live my life every day.

FOREWORD

He has shown you, O man, what is good;
and what does the LORD require of you but to do justly,
to love mercy, and to walk humbly with your God?

MICAH 6:8 NKJV

This book is a small glimpse into a few of the life lessons I've picked up on my journey, not only as a business leader, but much more importantly, as someone who loves God and desires to live for Him in all areas of my life. Of course I don't hold myself up as a perfect example for you to follow, but my prayer is that something I have experienced and recount in the following pages will impact you in a personal, positive, and powerful way.

In the scripture above, the prophet Micah keeps things simple by reminding us that what God requires is people who "act justly, love mercy and walk humbly with God." I'm not trying to break new ground. Instead, I want to provide reminders and put emphasis on basic life issues that have made a profound difference in my own life. I hope that my story can encourage you on the journey to better live, learn, and lead.

Are you ready to live a more positive and joyful life—not in the shadows of unhappiness and small-spiritedness, but in the sunlight of the marvelous gift of life you have received from God? Are you ready to learn more from your experiences—not just facts and head knowledge, but about how to take steps to reach your full potential? Are you ready to count for something in the hearts and lives of others through the way you lead—to positively impact the lives of those who see you in action every day?

I hope your answer to all three questions is yes, and that you will allow God to bless you while you live, learn, and lead in your corner of the world.

—DON SODERQUIST

PART 1

LIVE WITH PURPOSE

Not that I have already attained, or am already perfected;
but I press on, that I may lay hold of that
for which Christ Jesus has also laid hold of me.
PHILIPPIANS 3:12 NKJV

When I was a young man, I wanted to change the world.
I found it was difficult to change the world, so I tried to
change my nation. When I found I couldn't change the
nation, I began to focus on my town. I couldn't change the
town and as an older man, I tried to change my family.
Now, as an old man, I realize the only thing I can change
is myself, and suddenly I realize that if long ago I had
changed myself, I could have made an impact on my family.
My family and I could have made an impact on our town.
Their impact could have changed the nation and I could
indeed have changed the world.
—UNKNOWN MONK, A.D. 1100

HAVING A PERSONAL MISSION

....

Just think, you're here not by chance, but by God's choosing.
His hand formed you and made you the person you are.
He compares you to no one else—you are one of a kind.
You lack nothing that His grace can't give you.
He has allowed you to be here at this time in history
to fulfill His special purpose for this generation.

— ROY LESSIN

....

Some of you may be asking, "Could it really be true that there is a divinely-inspired purpose for my life? Me? I'm one of a kind? I lack nothing to accomplish what I am called to do? Sounds great, but certainly this must be for someone else. I don't feel that special. I'm just a normal human being trying to do my best each day. I wish it were true that I have a special mission. I really want to be more and do more, but …"

Don't doubt it for a moment. It is true! We all have been

gifted in so many ways. That means you and me. There is no question that we are different, but that doesn't mean that we don't have something significant to offer. What is important is that each of us realizes we have unique talents—and then decides to use those abilities for a greater good. Unfortunately, too many of us live our lives in dull routine. We don't come close to recognizing our full potential, to being the best we can be. We've stopped believing and dreaming.

A great joy in my life has been to see people grow and develop and become more than they ever dreamed they could be, to have a sense of direction they never felt before, and to achieve a greatness beyond their wildest expectation. I love that!

In the classic Lewis Carroll book, *Alice In Wonderland*, Alice begins an enchanted journey and comes to a fork in the road. She looks around for direction, sees the Cheshire Cat, and asks him, "Would you tell me, please, which way I ought to go from here?" He responds with a query of his own, "That depends a good deal on where you want to get to." She says, "I don't much care where." He famously answers, "Then it doesn't much matter which way you go."

That exchange alone tells us that the book is not just a simple children's story. There is an incredible lesson there for all of us; if we don't know where we want to go in life—or worse yet, don't care where we end up—it doesn't matter what choices we make.

Where do you want to go? What has God put on your heart to accomplish? When was the last time you asked yourself these questions?

It is essential that we take the time in our lives to decide where we want to go. And the question is not just for individuals. Organizations of all types and sizes must deal with the question of purpose on a regular and disciplined basis.

You are unique and gifted. That's a given. But where do you want to go? Who do you want to be when you grow up? What is your purpose?

When I retired from Walmart, I was determined to continue to make my life count and wanted to make a difference investing my life in something worthwhile. I wanted to impact people in a positive way, especially to encourage other leaders to be a positive influence in the lives of their people. So, together, with the help of trusted friends and family members, we started The Soderquist Center at John Brown University.

I was—and am—deeply concerned about the deterioration in ethical standards in our country; the blurring of right and wrong; the dilution of the biblically-based values that made our nation great. It was apparent to me that significant moral erosion was taking place rapidly in every corner of our modern culture—education, politics, sports, entertainment, churches, and families.

At the Center, when we meet with groups of leaders, we often ask them if they think that ethical behavior today is better, the same as, or worse than it was ten to fifteen years ago. The vast majority of the leaders (usually over 90%) say that their view of today's ethical behavior is that it is worse. Much worse. Many have suggested that we have lost our moral compass altogether.

Where and when do we put an end to this trend? Who is standing in the gap, doing all they can to turn things around—or to at least slow down the erosion? Where are the leaders of character and integrity?

I've strained so hard to hear their voices that I had to do something.

At The Soderquist Center, we have dedicated ourselves to raising yellow flags and even red flags with as many leaders as possible. We are attempting to have a transforming impact on the way people in business and other organizations think and lead. We are challenging leaders to determine what their personal mission really is, clearly articulate that mission to their people and build their organizations on a sound foundation of virtuous values. Anybody can talk about how politics or businesses are corrupt, or how they feel disgusted by the corruption they hear about on the news. We're trying to encourage people to do something about it.

We are passionate about making a difference. We specifically reach out to company leaders, not because of their titles, but because of the incredible influence that they have on so many people in their organizations. If we can reach CEOs and senior leaders, we have a much better chance of impacting their entire business and business culture. If we can have an impact on business, we likewise have a much better chance of making an impact on individuals and their families. If we can impact individuals and families, we can have an impact on society at large.

We are influencing emerging leaders with our message as well: college students, graduate students, and "high potential" individuals in organizations that have been recognized as having the potential to be the senior leaders of tomorrow. The response has been exciting. We are making a difference. We are seeing individual lives changed. We stay in touch with our participants and celebrate when we hear that these individuals are having an impact on those around them, including, and maybe most of all, in their families.

That's my purpose. That's what gets me up every morning with a smile on my face—whether I've had my first cup of coffee or not—ready to go to work, to battle. I'm supposed to be enjoying my retirement years—and I am! In fact, I love my work with leaders so much that I'm not sure it's really work. I'm convinced that what I do is so enjoyable because I am following my personal mission.

Are you facing a decision and contemplating which path to take? Well, where do you want to go?

....

For you have been called for this purpose,

since Christ also suffered for you,

leaving you an example for you to follow in His steps.

1 PETER 2:21 NASB

....

RECOGNIZING YOUR CREATOR

···

*For, after all, put it as we may to ourselves, we are all of us
from birth to death guests at a table which we did not spread.
The sun, the earth, love, friends, our very breath are parts of
the banquet. Shall we think of the day as a chance
to come nearer to our Host, and to find out something
of Him who has fed us so long?*

—REBECCA HARDING DAVIS

···

I was sitting on the shore of my favorite lake in
Wisconsin one autumn day. It is not a very big lake,
maybe twenty-five miles around, with a few small coves
and bays, but it is truly beautiful. The early settlers in this
part of Wisconsin decided that they would require all
the property owners around the lake to provide a public
access pathway on their property for those who would
like to hike any portion or even all the way around the
lake. That was a wise choice those settlers made so many

years ago. They were thinking about the many travelers who would come years later and be able to enjoy the beauty of the lake.

That raises a great question for you and me: Do we think about those coming after us and the kind of pathway we are leaving for them?

On weekends, hundreds of people of all ages enjoy the pilgrimage. Even on weekdays, scores and scores of people come to our lake to walk and enjoy the scenery. It has always been interesting to sit there, twenty to twenty-five feet away, and watch the people as they trek around the lake. Some walk, some run, some carry weights and swing their arms, and some walk with their dogs. Some keep their heads down and some look up to wave and say, "Hi." No two people are exactly alike. They are all different and unique.

As I was sitting there on that particular day, I was mesmerized by the sight of the deep blue water. I felt a soft gentle breeze and watched it create waves that rolled up onto the shore. It was so peaceful and relaxing. The sky was a little lighter blue and there were white puffy clouds lazily drifting by. The warmth of the sun seemed to sink into my whole being.

On the shore across from me, I looked at the beautiful green trees that had started to change to their fall colors. I really hadn't noticed before how many different kinds of trees there were. They were turning different shades of yellow, orange, and red. The colors blended together magnificently with the tall dark green pine trees.

As it grew later in the day, I watched the sun begin to set in the western sky. The clouds began turning their different shades of yellow, orange, pink, purple, and even red against the darkening blue sky. As time went by, all the colors became more brilliant and occasionally the sun would poke its bright orange head from behind the clouds as if to say, "I'm still here."

The gentle breeze stopped and the water became very calm, appearing almost like glass. What a magnificent scene! I took out my camera and snapped a few pictures but they really didn't compare with what I was watching. As I sat there, I wished that I were a painter so I could capture the moment. But I knew no matter how gifted I might be with brush and pallet in hand, I could never completely capture how these several hours made me feel. I felt that I had a moment where I was allowed to touch my Creator's hand.

I couldn't stop watching. The sky went from a bright royal blue to a rich azure and then melted into jet black. Millions of stars began to appear like diamonds, scattered across the heavens. The moon replaced the sun as the brightest light in the sky. Another day was done. But the wonder and majesty I experienced stayed with me.

In the days ahead, the leaves fell to the earth, leaving the trees without their brilliant colors. The days grew shorter and cooler and, eventually, pure white snow covered the green grass. As I reflected on what I had seen, I knew I had been looking through a small window into God's wonderful creation right from our front yard.

As I think of those special moments, I still stand in amazement.

The fantastic colors of this planet that we all call our home; the brilliance of a sunset; the changing of seasons that each bring their own beauty; the realization that the earth, stars, planets and moon are traveling in synchronized orbits around the sun and that they are just a tiny piece of our galaxy and the everyday miracles we witness; the realization that there are numerous other galaxies that all travel millions of miles per hour in perfect harmony … all I can say is, "Wow!" Oftentimes these thoughts make me feel so small in comparison to this vast, created expanse. Small in comparison, yes, but just as intricate and miraculous.

As I think about all the people who walked the shore path that day and for all those years before and after, I hope each and every one of them experienced at least a little of what I did. I hope I never forget that moment. No matter how very different we seem to be as people— the way we look, the way we talk, the way we think, the way we move, the way we act—we are still connected because we have been fashioned by the same Creator. Every one of us is just as dependent on every breath of air we take and every beat of our hearts to live.

Just as the heavens were created, so were we. The design of our universe—and the design of our being—is inescapable. But if you're like me, it often takes an illness or ailment to appreciate the complexity of our bodies: Our organs and anatomical systems function in perfect harmony. We are *fearfully and wonderfully made* (Psalm 139:14).

God has designed an incredible world and body for us to live in.

I could go on and on, but I've shared just a small taste of what I saw and felt in those few hours sitting by a lake in Wisconsin. What an incredible creation! In my mind, it takes much more faith to believe that this all happened by chance than to consider such an intricate design may be the handiwork of a master designer. In His wisdom, God has created a paradise for us to inhabit and preserve. I take so much of everyday life for granted and don't always remember to appreciate what God, our Creator has done.

How about you? Do you acknowledge that life is a gift from God?

Any counsel, any wisdom I have on living begins with the simple reminder to recognize our Creator with wonder and humility.

For thus says the Lord, Who created the heavens,
Who is God, Who formed the earth and made it,
Who has established it, Who did not create it in vain,
Who formed it to be inhabited:
"I am the Lord, and there is no other."

ISAIAH 45:18 NKJV

HAVING DETERMINATION

....

Nothing in this world can take the place of persistence.
Talent will not: nothing is more common
than unsuccessful men with talent. Genius will not;
unrewarded genius is almost a proverb.
Education will not: the world is full of educated derelicts.
Persistence and determination alone are omnipotent.

—CALVIN COOLIDGE

....

Every one of us will encounter difficulties and setbacks
in our lives. How do we handle them? Do we persevere?
Do we bounce back and try again?

One day, at The Soderquist Center's ropes course at
John Brown University, I was watching two participants
try to scale the fifty-foot climbing tower—no easy
feat. The first one shimmied right up the tower. After
watching her, I was so inspired; I thought I might be
able to zip up the tower myself!

The second participant, a little out of shape, grunted and groaned with every effort but it didn't appear there was any way he was going to make it up.

Everyone reacts differently if they fail to reach the top. Some just give up and accept that they can't do it. Others are relentless, trying two, three, four, even five more times to make it to the top. And even if they don't, many usually reach a higher mark than they did the first time—often higher than they had ever thought possible. Sure enough, the second participant persisted. And after his third attempt, he had made it all the way up. He shouted down to us on the ground about the magnificent view.

I saw a similar thing happen while watching the 2014 Winter Olympics. When U.S. figure skater Jeremy Abbott fell—and I don't just mean fell, but really smacked the ice hard—while attempting a difficult quadruple toe loop, my heart sank. I saw him slide into the sideboard, grimacing in pain, and thought, there is no way is he getting back up. No way. But he did. And he performed magnificently. His score suffered some, but he earned maybe the biggest ovation of the skating events.

Truly, the mark of an excellent person is not seen just in their accomplishments, but also in how they handle defeats. Our second participant could have given up right after his first failed attempt and sat down to rest in the shade. No one is forced to climb. Think of how easy that would have been.

There are countless examples of great people who persevered through difficulty, but the following may be one of the greatest:

In 1831, he failed in business.
In 1832, he was defeated for the state legislature.
In 1833, he failed in business again.
In 1834, he was elected to the state legislature.
In 1835, his fiancée died.
In 1836, he suffered a nervous breakdown.
In 1838, he was defeated for Speaker.
In 1840, he was defeated for elector.
In 1843, he was defeated for U.S. Congress.
In 1848, he lost re-nomination for U.S. Congress.
In 1855, he was defeated for the U.S. Senate.

In 1856, he was defeated for Vice President of the United States.
In 1858, he was defeated for the U.S. Senate.
In 1861, he was elected as the sixteenth President of the United States.

Abraham Lincoln is widely recognized as one of the greatest presidents in American history. And what a model of determination he is to all of us who have struggled on the way to achieving a goal.

When I first heard the Walmart story from beginning to end, I was surprised to learn that Sam Walton, the highly successful founder of the company and later-to-be richest man in the world, unexpectedly lost the lease on his first store. But he didn't let a setback like losing his first building stop him. Sam quickly found a new store location and set up shop all over again. It made me wonder, *what if Sam had given up on owning his own store after losing that first lease?* In hindsight, we may now scoff at the thought that the world's largest company could have failed because of a single lease. But with a fledgling business venture and the risk of failure looming, giving up would have been a much more common response. If Sam had given up—and few would have called him crazy for doing so—no doubt the world would be a different place today. I know my life would have been different and I would have missed being part of an incredible story.

How do you respond to setbacks in life, whether at work, in your family or in your personal life? Do you shut down in the face of disappointment? Do you look to jump ship when things get difficult? Or, do you dig a little deeper in your soul and find the strength to overcome? Be assured that no worthwhile endeavor will be without pain and disappointment.

Of course, I can't promise you that the next time you endure a struggle, it will pay off like it did for Abraham Lincoln or for Sam Walton. But remember our second climber at the ropes course. Now, everyone may not think that his struggle and perseverance was worth it. But I know he did. I can still hear him shouting down to us victoriously after he had made it to the top. He said he could see for miles.

What challenges are you facing right now? What

obstacle do you need to overcome? Are you tempted to give up?

I pray you'll keep climbing. I don't want you to miss the view from the top.

....

But you, brothers and sisters,
never become tired of doing good.

2 THESSALONIANS 3:13 NCV

....

LIVE WITH PURPOSE BY...

EXPRESSING GRATITUDE

....

*Thank God every morning when you get up that you
have something to do which must be done, whether you like it
or not. Being forced to work, and forced to do your best,
will breed in you temperance, self-control, diligence,
strength of will, content, and a hundred other virtues
which the idle never know.*

—CHARLES KINGSLEY

....

We've all seen children who are never satisfied with what
they have. They pout, whine, and complain because they
want a new toy or more candy. When we see these children,
at the grocery store or elsewhere, we might roll our eyes and
wonder to ourselves about the way their parents are raising
them. We might feel relief that it is someone else's kids or
grandkids this time and not our own.

But one thing worse than seeing a spoiled child
act up is interacting with a thankless grown-up. They

probably don't scream or hold their breath until they faint in order to get what they want, but it's terrible to be around them. They seem to take everything they have for granted. I know rich people like this, and they are miserable in the midst of their wealth and belongings.

I know that in a free market society, workers have the right to negotiate the best compensation deal possible for themselves. But I have to tell you, nothing turns me off more than to watch multi-millionaire professional athletes try to look wounded and defrauded during contract negotiations. Again, I know they have the right to maximize their earnings, but their situation feels so alien to the average working man or woman.

Bottom line: it is clear that few things will diminish your life more quickly and profoundly than being ungrateful.

Conversely, nothing will enlarge your life more quickly and dramatically than gratitude. I know poor people who are convinced they are rich.

I went on a trip to Nigeria to speak to government officials, business leaders, and bankers. While there, I saw people who truly had nothing. Yet they savored their simple blessings. And they were the happiest people I saw. What the Nigerians taught me through their gratefulness in poverty impacted me more than anything I could ever hope to leave behind with them. They showed me that being grateful for what you have will cure anger, bitterness, resentment, jealousy, low self-esteem, and a quarreling spirit.

In the 100th Psalm—a Bible passage we should all take to heart—King David leads the people of his nation in worship of God. Not only does he tell them to have a thankful attitude in their hearts, he also says that they must say it aloud. "Give thanks." David knows the real reasons for gratitude:

- We have been created by God and belong to Him (100:3).
- The Lord is good and His love endures forever (100:5).

Does being created by God and having God's enduring love mean that everything went right for David? Hardly. His life was loaded with heartache and disappointment.

He often lived in a state of depression and near despair. David's own son, Absalom, turned against him and tried to kill him. Still, he understood that even in the "valley of the shadow of death" (Psalm 23:4), God was always near to comfort, bless, and deliver him from danger.

How often do you slow down to think about how blessed your life really is? Do you look at your world with eyes of wonder and appreciation? With thankfulness?

A thankful heart leads to an enriched life. David's life is a great reminder that, even in the midst of challenges—for us, they may be in our work, our home, our relationships, or our personal development—the thankful heart realizes that God's love and provision and care is immeasurable.

When is the last time you wrote out a list of all the things for which you are thankful?

Oh, give thanks to the Lord, for He is good!
For His mercy endures forever.

1 CHRONICLES 16:34 NKJV

KEEPING A SENSE OF HUMOR

....

Those who bring sunshine into the lives of others
cannot keep it from themselves.

—JAMES MATTHEW BARRIE

....

As I write this, Jimmy Fallon is the buzz of the entertainment industry. He took over for Jay Leno who was host of the Tonight Show for twenty years. But I go back further than that.

Johnny Carson will always be the king of late-night talk in my estimation. He entertained me and millions of Americans at bedtime for over twenty-five years. We never got tired of watching him, probably because his best material wasn't scripted, but rather a spontaneous interaction with his guests. No matter what they had to say, he could always turn it into something funny and entertaining. Not many people could do what Carson was able to do on that program, but everyone can have a sense of humor.

I don't remember the best jokes I've heard, and even when I do, I don't tell them that well. But you don't have to be a comedian to benefit from humor. The writer of Proverbs tells us: "A merry heart does good, like medicine" (17:22). So I laugh, smile, tease, and tell jokes poorly all the same. I try to enjoy the lighter side of life.

Yes, life is serious and we can't joke around all the time. But that doesn't mean we always have to be somber. In *Man's Search for Meaning*, Viktor E. Frankl, a Jewish neurologist and psychiatrist from Austria and survivor of the Auschwitz death camp, teaches us that one of the keys to mental health and experiencing life fully is laughter. I believe him. Anyone that can survive a death camp and still teach the value of laughter has immense credibility in my eyes.

In my Walmart days, we worked hard. But we always had fun. I can tell you that work and fun are not mutually exclusive. Sam Walton was great at using humor and wasn't afraid to poke a little fun at himself, too. If sales were soft or we were going through a difficult time, Sam would lead a crazy sing-along or a talent show at our Saturday morning managers' meeting to liven everyone up. In 1984, Sam even did a hula dance on Wall Street in response to our associates' achievement of a particularly high year-end goal. The press went wild over Sam's outrageous performance at the time. I am amazed that people still ask me about it today.

Of course, some smirked and made fun of what they thought was a simple publicity stunt. I have to believe that they simply didn't know the kind of man Sam was: A man of total integrity who knew how to motivate people to achieve a goal nobody thought was possible. His hula dance was more than humor. It showed me and everyone else at Walmart that Sam was completely prepared to hold up his end of a deal. He made a promise and kept it. His associates loved it. The performance built up morale, and he enjoyed a good laugh. Humor was a part of my everyday life in Walmart and I think it made us much more effective.

In my judgment, Ronald Reagan was extraordinarily effective with his humor. It was often in response to a criticism, sometimes self-deprecating. His humor was disarming. Even his opponents struggled to keep a straight face.

When he was accused of not working hard, he quipped, "Hard work never killed anyone, but why take the chance."

When he felt like the media wasn't recognizing his administration's accomplishments, he said, "It's my job to solve all the problems in the world and it's your job to make sure nobody finds out about it."

As governor of California, he saw a student protester that appeared to be spaced out on drugs carrying a sign that read, "Make love, not war." Reagan quipped to one of his aides: "I'm not sure he's in shape to do either one of those things."

One of his most defining moments of turning to humor as a great defense and offense was during the 1984 presidential debates when asked if, at 73, he was too old to be President. His classic response was: "I will not make age an issue of this campaign. I am not going to exploit, for political purposes, my opponent's youth and inexperience." Not even Michael Dukakis, his opponent in the debate, could keep from laughing.

The stories of his classic wit can fill a book. Just note, the man who had the most powerful position in the world wielded humor with incredible grace and success.

I hope humor is part of your life, too. It takes a positive attitude and a strong desire to enjoy life to see the humor around us, but having a little laughter sprinkled throughout your day is a great way to live.

....

A merry heart does good, like medicine,
but a broken spirit dries the bones.

PROVERBS 17:22 NKJV

....

BEING OPTIMISTIC

....

The essence of optimism is that it takes no account of the present,
but it is a source of inspiration, of vitality and hope
where others have resigned; it enables a man
to hold his head high, to claim the future for himself
and not to abandon it to his enemy.

—DIETRICH BONHOEFFER

....

Being optimistic means having a positive "can do" attitude. And attitude has a major impact on what you accomplish in life. So, it's no surprise that many successful people think optimistically and believe they can influence the outcome of the circumstances of their lives. Optimistic people say to themselves, "I can do it. And, in fact, I will do it."

Henry Ford is credited with the great quote: "If you think you can or you think you can't, you are right."

Every year at Walmart, we had a different annual theme. One year, our theme was "Imagine the Possible." In preparation for my presentation to all our store managers about the new theme, I thought about the two words we had debated using: "possible" versus "impossible."

Having gone back and forth between the two words, I was reminded of the importance of our vernacular. Our language reflects our thinking and affects our behavior. Sam maintained an optimism that pushed those around him to think and speak about what might be possible: imagine the possible. On the other hand, I believe that our competitors encountered limitations in achievement because they thought and spoke differently. In some cases, they simply failed to actively explore the boundaries of possibility. Were we more intelligent? No. Were we better resourced? No. So as I spoke that year to our store managers, I remarked on what struck me about the definition of impossible.

In my copy of the Merriam-Webster Dictionary, *impossible* is defined as: "Felt to be incapable of being done, attained, or fulfilled." The phrase in this definition that jumped off the page at me was "felt to be." In other words, the definition of impossible doesn't necessarily mean that it can't be done, but that the task doesn't *seem* probable to the person considering it. The label *impossible* is a restriction we place on ourselves, a surefire way to self-sabotage our full potential. As author, activist, and lawyer Charles Chestnutt said, "Impossibilities are merely things of which we have not learned, or which we do not wish to happen."

There have been many events in history that were perceived to be impossible but have been accomplished after all.

In the 1950s, two Harvard scientists conclusively proved that space travel was impossible because of the weight of the fuel and fuel tanks needed to create sufficient boost. That conclusion was emphatically disproved a decade later when the United States landed men on the moon and got them back to Earth safely.

Performing a heart transplant seemed like science fiction when I was growing up. Even in the medical community when a few forward-thinking researchers ventured to conceive of it, most of their colleagues wrote it off as impossible. But Dr. Christian Bernard of

South Africa performed the surgery for the first time in 1967—successfully—and today, doctors all over the world are transplanting organs all the time, not just hearts.

Think about the creation of Disneyland and Disney World. A major, national theme park concept was a new and risky undertaking. *Would people really want to travel to a theme park full of cartoon characters? How bizarre.* When Walt Disney unveiled his vision, there were plenty of naysayers. But Disney succeeded and created a completely new kind of entertainment experience that has even changed the travel patterns of tourists from across the globe. He built vacation paradises on both coasts of the U.S., in Europe, and in Asia.

When Fred Smith, founder of Federal Express, came up with the idea of sending a package from anywhere in the country to someone in any other city overnight, not many believed it could be done. In fact, one of his business professors gave him a low grade for his business plan, which Fred first wrote as a class assignment, citing feasibility issues. Now Federal Express is one of the most common means of shipping for individuals and businesses in our country and around the globe. We can't imagine a world where we would have to wait more than a couple of days to get a package we needed.

All of these achievements were perceived to be impossible when they were introduced. Still, somehow they were accomplished. Surely, behind each of them were people who refused to label their plans impossible.

The minister and author Norman Vincent Peale writes, "Become a possibilitarian. No matter how dark things seem to be or actually are, raise your sights and see possibilities—always see them, for they're always there."

The writer of the New Testament letter to the Hebrews framed this in terms of faith when he wrote: "Now faith is the substance of things hoped for, the evidence of things not seen" (11:1 NKJV).

Ultimately, optimism is the exercise of faith. It is believing that what is invisible, what seems impossible, or what seems to be too daunting, can actually be.

Are there challenges in your life that seem too tough? Are there expectations placed on you that you consider unattainable? It's not for me to say what you can and can't do. If you believe that things are possible in a world where many don't, you can open up the boundaries of your mind. Who knows what you may be able to do?

…If you have faith as a mustard seed, you will say to this mountain, "Move from here to there," and it will move; and nothing will be impossible for you.

MATTHEW 17:20 NKJV

LIVE WITH PURPOSE BY...

LOVING OTHERS

....

We should never leave love at the door when we

come to work. On the contrary, love works.

—@JOELMANBY

....

Does love permeate your life? I'm not talking about
an emotional state of feeling happy or having general
affection. I'm talking about an active lifestyle—a posture
of interest, care, and kindness. I'm talking about an active
love of God and love for others.

If you graduated from an Ivy League school with
the highest honors, but don't have love in your life, do
your educational credentials fulfill you completely?
If you started your own successful business, or took a
high-paying job with a Fortune 500 company, but don't
have love in your life, would your impressive business
accomplishments be enough to make you truly happy?
If you invent the next big mobile app or social media

site, but don't have love in your life, does your brilliance really matter?

I'm asking these questions after having seen many people become incredibly successful. They are the top in their field of academia. They are serial entrepreneurs or top executives at Fortune 500 companies who have become very wealthy. They have published books with great acclaim. They take elaborate vacations and have enormous houses. But it is so clear that many of the people who seem to have everything are still missing something in their lives. They aren't happy. They aren't joyful.

They have missed out on the simple lesson from the great 20th Century German psychoanalyst, Erik Erikson, who said of children—and all of us—that they want to "love and be loved." It doesn't get much simpler than that.

The great Lebanese philosopher and poet, Khalil Gibran gave great advice when he wrote: "If you cannot work with love but only with distaste, it is better that you should leave your work."

We live in a society that lets values get turned upside down and lets priorities slide out of whack. We love money and use people to get it. We crave more time and space for ourselves, but live in disconnected, lonely families. We chase after possessions so much that instead of owning them, they own us.

When a religious leader asked Jesus to distill the absolute, number one, most important commandment, He answered by saying:

> ...'You shall love the Lord your God with all your heart, with all your soul, and with all your mind.' This is the first and great commandment. And the second is like it: 'You shall love your neighbor as yourself.'
> (Matthew 22:37-39 NKJV)

When Paul wrote his letter to the Corinthian church, apparently a group of new Christians who were quite proud of their sophisticated culture, intelligence, and spiritual gifts, he said to them:

> Though I speak with the tongues of men and of angels, but have not love, I have become sounding brass or a

*clanging cymbal. And though I have the gift of prophesy,
and understand all mysteries and all knowledge,
and though I have all faith, so that I could remove
mountains, but have not love, I am nothing*
(1 Corinthians 13:1-2 NKJV).

The associates at Walmart loved and respected
Sam Walton. Why? Because he made everyone feel
important, from the home office to the local store. One
of the first things he did on store visits was ask the
cashiers how they were doing. He lived so that everyone
around him could see and feel the love in his life. Sam
was able to lead the company to new heights again and
again. I believe it's because the associates loved and
trusted him.

But going one step back, I believe that his associates
loved and trusted him, because Sam loved and trusted
them. They could feel it and they could see it.

Living a life of love is about loving people. But Steve
Jobs made a very interesting observation when he said
we need to love what we do for a living as well:

Your work is going to fill a large part of your life, and the only way to be truly satisfied is to do what you believe is great work. And the only way to do great work is to love what you do. If you haven't found it yet, keep looking. Don't settle. As with all matters of the heart, you'll know when you find it. And, like any great relationship, it just gets better and better as the years roll on.

What we know, the things we own, the job we have, and the prestige we have accrued, are all not enough to bring meaning and satisfaction into our lives. Out of the mouths of Jesus and Paul, we hear the same message: Loving God and your neighbor are the most important things you can do, and nothing can replace them. Living greatly follows loving greatly.

And now abide faith, hope, love, these three; but the greatest of these is love.

1 CORINTHIANS 13:13 NKJV

DOING THINGS RIGHT

I've met a few people in my time who were enthusiastic about hard work. And it was just my luck that all of them happened to be men I was working for at the time.

—BILL GOLD

I'm not what you'd call a cowpoke, but I was inspired one day when I heard the famous Texas cowboy poet, Red Steagall, quote his poem, "The Fence that Me and Shorty Built." It's a poem about a very young would-be cowboy who is asked to help build a fence. He thinks fence-building is beneath him, since he was hired to drive cattle and rope steers. And so, just as he begrudgingly starts digging postholes, he starts cutting corners. He goes around the rocks rather than digging them up and finds other ways to make the job easier. As the rest of the crew starts setting posts, Shorty, the wise old cowboy who is also the foreman, notices that the fence zigs and zags haphazardly. It's definitely not straight, the way they marked it out. So he pulls our young cowpoke aside for a talk and says:

Now we could let it go like this
And take the easy route.
But doin' things the easy way
Ain't what it's all about.

If you're not proud of what you do,
You won't amount to much.
You'll bounce around from job to job
Just slightly out of touch.

Shorty convinces the cowboy to go back and fix his mistakes. He reminds him that not only will he save his job today, but on another day, years from now, he'll ride by and see a straight, durable fence and be able to point with pride to his work.

All of us have assignments, jobs, and responsibilities that we don't enjoy as much as others—that don't bring us as much immediate benefit as others. Still, like the cowboy in the poem, we have a lot to learn from difficult, less rewarding jobs:

- Do whatever you're asked to do. No job is so small or menial that it doesn't need to be done well. And no one is too good for those small jobs.
- Do things right the first time. If you don't have time to do a job once, you certainly don't have time to do it again.
- Your attitude affects everyone around you. Attitude is contagious, and a positive attitude can make the difference between a task completed with excellence and one done with shoddy workmanship.
- Take pride in what you do. Remember, your name is on every "fence" you build. Do your best in everything, so that you can look back on your work with pride.
- Go back and correct your mistakes. We all make mistakes. The wise person admits them, corrects them, and doesn't leave them for others to clean up.

Legendary Green Bay Packer coach, Vince Lombardi, put it this way:

> *Winning is not a sometime thing; it's an all time thing. You don't win once in a while, you don't do things right once in a while, you do them right all the time. Winning is habit. Unfortunately, so is losing.*

What about you? Are you working with excellence in all areas of your work and life? Or are you slacking on those jobs you don't enjoy as much as others? Can you look back on everything you've done in the past six months with pride? Anything you wish you could do over? Ultimately, are you committed to doing great work in all areas of your life?

Remember: "Doin' things the easy way ain't what it's all about."

....

Whatever your hand finds to do, do it with all your might.

ECCLESIASTES 9:10 NKJV

....

CHOOSING TO BE JOYFUL

....

Joy does not simply happen to us.
We have to choose joy and keep choosing it every day.

—HENRI J.M. NOUWEN

....

I was sitting at the kitchen table in my home, jotting down a few thoughts for a section of this book and half-listening to the news that was airing on the TV in another room—a mixture of shocking catastrophes: A terrible earthquake in the Philippines; a teenager who had opened fire on fellow students at his high school; lawsuits and counter lawsuits within a family over ongoing life support measures. *Whew. Heavy stuff*, I thought to myself. *Life can be so hard and unfair.* I had to sigh.

I was distracted from writing for now. But as I stood up, I saw a plaque that my wife had recently put up on the wall in front of me. On it were two simple words: *Scatter Joy.*

I sat back down and asked myself, *do I scatter joy? Do I even understand true joy?*

Of course, I understand happiness and talk about it a lot. My family and I certainly have many reasons to be happy. But happiness is based on circumstances. I know too well that I'm not as happy when things aren't going the way I want them to go. *But am I joyful?*

Joy is not based on circumstances. You can experience a deep, abiding joy no matter what you have to be happy or unhappy about in your world. Joyful people radiate something deeper, something based in their heart and will. Others sense this joy and feel uplifted. I realized that's what the phrase *Scatter Joy* is all about—reflecting that deep and abiding joy to the world. And I realized that I couldn't heed the sign at all without being joyful myself.

How much true joy do you see on a typical day in your life? I know it's easy to spot people who appear to be joyless. They look absolutely miserable in traffic. They shake their fists, yell, and blast their car horns. When someone in front of them at the convenience store is moving a little slow, they mutter, scowl, and shift on their feet. I even see these luckless people at church, singing hymns about God's amazing grace, looking like they have just swallowed a lemon.

How about you? Do you want to live to make a difference? If so, you have to be different than those who go with the flow. Seek joy. It is all around those who seek God.

The joy of God's presence. In Psalms 16:8-9 (NCV), David exalts: "I keep the Lord before me always. Because he is close by my side, I will not be hurt. So I rejoice and am glad." If God is beside you, no one can steal that joy.

The joy of God's goodness. Isaiah 63:9 tells us of God's great redemptive work: "In all their affliction He was afflicted, And the Angel of His Presence saved them; In His love and in His pity He redeemed them; And He bore them and carried them all the days of old" (NKJV). What a kind and good God Isaiah describes—the same God we have today. What a reason to be joyful.

The joy of God's Word. King David speaks of God's Word with awe, reverence, and joy: "I delight to do Your will, O my God, and Your law is within my heart" (Psalm

40:8 NKJV). Do you set yourself up for joy each day by partaking of God's Word—reading the Bible?

The joy of a clean heart. One of the most beautiful prayers ever uttered was David's contrite prayer for cleansing: "Create in me a pure heart, God, and make my spirit right again. Do not send me away from you or take your Holy Spirit away from me. Give me back the joy of your salvation. Keep me strong by giving me a willing spirit" (Psalms 51:10-12 NCV). Joy comes from seeking God's forgiveness and cleansing.

The joy in suffering. It doesn't seem possible to experience joy in the midst of sorrow, but Jesus reminded His disciples, "In the world you will have tribulation; but be of good cheer, I have overcome the world" (John 16:33 NKJV).

Sometimes it takes a decision, an act of the will, a step of faith, to be joyful—and then God can plant something real and abiding in our hearts.

....

Rejoice in the Lord always. Again I will say, rejoice!

PHILIPPIANS 4:4 NKJV

....

KEEPING HUMBLE

···

A great man is always willing to be little.

—RALPH WALDO EMERSON

···

It was the August after I'd joined Walmart, and I was about to get my first lesson in the ways of Sam Walton. We were opening three stores in Huntsville, Alabama. The company had acquired two stores from another chain on opposite sides of the city. Not knowing we were going to acquire that company, we had already purchased land in the center of Huntsville and had built a Walmart store there. Now we were on our way to participate in the grand opening of all three stores on the same day.

Sam went to the north store and I went to the south store. He cut the ribbon on the north and I cut the ribbon on the south. We met at the store in the center of town. We greeted customers, toured the store, and shook hands with associates. The store looked great and we wanted to thank our associates for doing such an excellent job.

Like most of the grand openings, we expected a big crowd, but in this one our productivity couldn't keep up with the traffic flow. Before long, Sam jumped in and began to bag merchandise, I handed out candy to the kids, and we did anything we could think of to help the customers feel more comfortable with the long lines.

Sam got on the PA repeatedly, asking the customers, "Anybody need anything?" He would then continue, "We are so sorry that you are being held up today. Next week things will settle down and the lines won't be so long. Thank you for coming to our grand opening today and being patient with us." He would then make a beeline to someone who needed help.

I have to confess, as the former president of a national retail chain and now an executive vice president for Walmart, I had never served customers on the front lines like I did that day. You don't think I was going to go to lunch while my supervisor bagged merchandise, do you?

Sam was a very humble man, and he taught me a valuable lesson that day. No one is too good to do the little jobs. He made me realize that there are no little jobs. If the Chairman of the Board wasn't too high and mighty to hand out lollipops and bag goods, neither was I.

There is a lot of talk these days about being a servant leader, but I'm afraid that there's much more talk than action. Our actions are the only things that really count. No matter how large Walmart became, Sam always reminded us that we were no better than anyone else, that we should never become blinded by our own importance. He maintained that example throughout his leadership.

A potential danger of being a leader is that we can begin to think that we have all of the answers. After all, we have achieved an important position, we think, and we're above taking advice and doing those so-called "little" jobs. I have seen too many leaders develop a large ego. Well, large egos frequently lead to arrogance, and when people become arrogant, their judgment can become impaired. Impaired judgment usually leads to failure.

We can see many examples of humility in the Scriptures. It is clear in Christ's teachings and in His life that we are to be humble people and put others before ourselves. When we follow Jesus' instructions in humility, we honor God, which is of the highest importance. And as a bonus we also live a life of purpose and fulfillment.

By the way, in the process of having fun and helping customers on that crazy day in Huntsville, I learned another life lesson I'll never forget. Humility is a marvelous partner to joy. I hope you will discover the joy of serving others.

....

Whoever desires to become great among you,

let him be your servant.

MATTHEW 20:26 NKJV

....

LIVING YOUR VALUES

*It's not hard to make decisions
when you know what your values are.*

—ROY DISNEY

There is much discussion over values today. Some would say we're practically at war over our values. The debate permeates entertainment, politics, religion, education, media—every arena of life. What's the big deal about values? Are my personal values really important?
I frequently ask leaders if they know what their personal values are, and most say yes. Then I ask them: "Have you ever written them down?" Most say no.

I looked the word *values* up in numerous dictionaries, and they were all a little different. The definition that best describes what I'm trying to say went like this: "The beliefs that people have about what is right and wrong and what is most important in life, which control their behavior."

Therefore, values are incredibly important! They determine who we really are—what our character is, the real you when the mask is off.

Where do our values come from? I know for myself that there has been a lifetime of influences that have shaped who I am—the values I hold. It began with my mom and dad, who were God-fearing people. They weren't any better than you or I, but they taught me what was right and wrong simply by what they said and how they lived. Their life lessons weren't complicated. It's wrong to lie, cheat, and steal. You should treat others the way you would like to be treated. They also taught me that there was a God who loved me—that I should love Him and follow His directions as found in the Bible. They taught me that there were consequences if I did wrong.

The interesting thing was that my teachers in school, my friends, relatives, and neighbors, my Sunday school teachers, my pastor, and basically everyone I knew believed pretty much the same things. And when I went to study at Wheaton College, my values and beliefs were once again reinforced by what I heard and saw there.

I realize that not everyone growing up when I did had the same reinforcement, but many did.

Now, I don't want you to think that my upbringing was perfect—it wasn't. I was naïve about things like discrimination when horrible examples of it existed just minutes from my hometown. I was unaware of the grinding hardship that plagues the lives of minorities. And my ignorance was wrong. I saw prejudice from a distance and chose not to get involved. I see things more clearly today, and I am pleased to observe that we have made progress as a nation. Still, we have a long way to go. Growing in my understanding and compassion in the area of prejudice has strengthened my values.

Other life experiences—seeing others suffer, the mistreatment of people in the workplace, the cold indifference and lack of compassion for those in need that we all exhibit when we are at our lowest—have reinforced many of my early learnings from my parents about treating everyone with respect and dignity.

And I'm still learning. I hope I never stop.

What I think is most important to understand is that the real key to sound values in our lives isn't so much what we say. The heart of our values is in what we do and how we do it. In other words, how are we living our lives? We can talk all we want, but the bottom line is who we are through what we do every day.

But respect Christ as the holy Lord in your hearts. Always be ready to answer everyone who asks you to explain about the hope you have, but answer in a gentle way and with respect. Keep a clear conscience so that those who speak evil of your good life in Christ will be made ashamed.

1 PETER 3:15-16 NCV

PART 2

LEARN AS A WAY OF LIFE

And do not be conformed to this world, but be transformed by the renewing of your mind, that you may prove what is that good and acceptable and perfect will of God.

ROMANS 12:2 NKJV

A child-like man is not a man whose development has been arrested; on the contrary, he is a man who has given himself a chance of continuing to develop long after most adults have muffled themselves in the cocoon of middle-aged habit and convention.

—ALDOUS HUXLEY

FEELING A SENSE OF WONDER

....

He who can no longer pause to wonder and stand rapt
in awe, is as good as dead; his eyes are closed.

—ALBERT EINSTEIN

....

Having grandchildren is wonderful. They help my wife and me keep a sense of wonder when we see their eyes light up over the littlest things.

To the very young, the beautiful wrapping paper on Christmas presents is almost as much fun as the presents themselves. It is delightful to see their rapt attention as they follow a line of tiny ants trooping across the sidewalk and down a little dirt hole. I have cherished moments of seeing my grandkids perched on their tippy-toes to catch snowflakes on their tongues, squinting as snow falls in their eyes.

As we grow older, we lose that wonder and awe over not only the little things, but also significant wonders of our world. The changing of the seasons. The sunrises and sunsets. Fresh fallen snow on evergreen branches. Birds chirping and mist rising up from the meadows on a cold frosty morning. Newly-tilled fields, planted in neat rows. The children I saw in Tokyo who stopped to pick up fallen cherry blossoms and throw them high in the air, just to wait for them to flicker back down to the ground.

In Michael Yaconelli's *Dangerous Wonder*, he shows us a beautiful picture of the awe he knew as a child and how, one day, it left him.

> *When I was six years old, my favorite comic book character was Superman. I admired his strength, his X-ray vision, his colorful uniform and bright red cape. What captured my imagination most was Superman's ability to fly. Many of my childhood fantasies were about flying. I honestly believed flying was still a possibility. I would talk my friends into playing Superman, and they would play for a while, but soon they would tire of the game because I wouldn't let anyone else be Superman. I had to be Superman, I told them, because I knew more about flying than they did.*

Sneaking into my parents' bathroom, I would find the stash of forbidden towels (the thick, new ones reserved only for guests). Once outside, with the towel tied around my neck and dragging on the dirt behind me, I would run as fast as I could and jump off the highest survivable launching pad I could find. With arms outstretched, cape billowing behind me, wind rushing past my ears, I believed I was flying.

Then came a day when, without warning, without provocation, I woke up, never to wear a "cape" again. Wherever the knowledge came from, it came nonetheless, and from that moment on I knew flying was nothing more than a childhood fantasy. I would never fly…and there is no Superman.

In retrospect, my day of "enlightenment" was a very sad day. I know now that something inside of me died that day. Whatever the "something" was, it was the stuff of dreams and imagination—the place where dancing, singing, laughter, and playing lived. Even at six, I understood that the possibility of flying wasn't the point: it was the aliveness I felt when I thought I could fly; it was the voice I heard *deep inside—a warm and loving voice, a living, believing voice, I recognized who it was: God. But that day, when I was just six years young my God-hearing went bad.*

How do you restore a spirit of wonder in your life? I think the most effective way is to simply watch a group of kids and see how they interact with each other and look at the world.

It is so easy to get wrapped up in the immediate concerns of life. And while I'm not against working hard, our busy lives can block out the wonderful things around us in nature, in food, in the stories of others. As you work hard on your journey to success, don't leave behind your ability to appreciate life's simple and profound pleasures.

How do you slow down to experience wonder?

Many, O Lord my God, are Your wonderful works which You have done; And Your thoughts toward us cannot be recounted to You in order; If I would declare and speak of them, they are more than can be numbered.

PSALM 40:5 NKJV

EVALUATING YOURSELF HONESTLY

....

One must not hold one's self so divine as to be unwilling

occasionally to make improvements in one's creations.

—LUDWIG VAN BEETHOVEN

....

I saw a couple of teenage girls at a store not too long ago. Their heads were bent close as they giggled and whispered together. Amused and curious, I looked in the direction that one of the girls pointed and sure enough, there were some nice looking boys their age standing around.

It is a natural part of the human mind to evaluate almost everything we see. And though the process of evaluating doesn't always look like it did for those girls snickering about the two boys, we all evaluate musicians, athletes, our pastors, our bosses, and the people we work with.

Most of us are evaluated at our places of employment. Whether we ever stop to think about it or not, everybody that we know or even come in contact with forms thoughts about us on the basis of what they hear us say and see us do.

But as natural as it is to size each other up, do we ever take the time to do the same for ourselves? That's hard to do—we're really not very objective about ourselves. And yet, self-evaluation can be incredibly valuable in growing as a person and as a leader.

If we have a genuine desire to be the best that we can be, the self-evaluation process begins by honestly taking a time-intensive look at ourselves and determining what we are doing well and what we could do better. Don't expect this to be possible in fifteen minutes, squeezed into a busy schedule in your office. You have to get away from the phone, computer, and everyone else, preferably in some restful place where you can do some serious, uninterrupted thinking. If you are married—and bold enough—ask your husband or wife to share their thoughts with you as a part of your preparation for a self-evaluation retreat. (Obviously, don't ask them right after or during an argument!)

Once you've reached some conclusions about your effectiveness, you have to decide what you need to do to improve, what you are willing to do, and how you can measure your success in the future.

We all have our strengths—and knowing these strengths can be a good way to understand how you can be most effective—but no one is perfect. Every one of us can improve. And to get to a real understanding of what we have to improve, we must be willing to honestly evaluate ourselves and follow that knowledge with a will to change. That's not easy—change is hard. In fact, change is very hard.

The 360-Degree Evaluation is no longer new, but it's still a relatively young development in the field of human resources. A lot of companies now use a 360-feedback tool for employee reviews. Instead of just having the boss rate an employee, feedback is given by peers, subordinates, and supervisors within the person's work circle. Sometimes a component that includes self-evaluation is thrown into the mix. The strength of the system is obvious. You can better plot changes and set goals when you have honest multi-directional feedback to work with.

At Walmart, we were constantly evaluating everything we did and looking for ways to improve. We didn't shy away from making major changes if that's what the company needed. We called this process "Correction of Errors." Even after very successful holiday seasons, we would spend only a few minutes celebrating the good things that we did. We spent the majority of our time determining what we could do better.

Periodic self-evaluation is very healthy for every one of us, just like going to the doctor for an annual physical. You can catch things that are going wrong and take appropriate corrective action before they become more serious.

Recognize that self-evaluation is not easy. Even more challenging is finding the determination to change aspects of our lives. As a person of faith, I believe that God expects the very best of us.

The good news is that the willingness to evaluate yourself means that you have the humility and honesty to reach the next level in your life. The even better news is that you don't have to do it on your own. God is always ready to hear our prayers and help us in our areas of need.

Here's a little list of questions I like to use to do my self-evaluations. Give it a try for your next one.

CHECK YOUR COORDINATES:

1. How effective are you as a leader? Rate yourself on a scale of 1-10.
2. Are you passionate about what you do and how you do it?
3. Can you see meaningful results from your efforts this past year? What are they?
4. Have you genuinely impacted someone this past year? Who and how?
5. Are you really happy in what you do?
6. Do you feel fulfilled? Do you feel a sense of accomplishment?
7. Could you be a better leader?

God began doing a good work in you,
and I am sure he will continue it until it is finished
when Jesus Christ comes again.

PHILIPPIANS 1:6 NCV

LISTENING

Courage is what it takes to stand up and speak;

courage is also what it takes to sit down and listen.

—WINSTON CHURCHILL

Peter MacMahon, a Walmart executive in Europe, told me about the following incident that happened when he was a young manager for a major retail conglomerate in England. I couldn't say it any better than he does in his story about the importance of listening.

I was working for Lewis's, one of the biggest departmental store groups in the UK. The shopping habits of the British consumer had changed in the previous decade, and our stores suffered sales and profit declined consistently for ten years.

I was in charge of the food division in the Manchester store in 1980, and was under constant pressure to reduce costs. I had decided to terminate a particular elevator operator in the goods receiving area.

David Flowers, who had operated the same goods elevator for thirty years, was, due to decreasing volumes, no longer required, and the plan was to let him go and close down the elevator he operated. On a Friday morning, the HR manager and I interviewed David and informed him his employment would be terminated and he would be compensated in line with company policy. He was devastated. I just considered it to be a necessary part of the job.

He left that Friday evening and took his personal belongings with him. On the following Monday, David came to work and was seen by members of the staff at his normal start time and duly proceeded to operate his lift. I was on leave that day so I had no part in how the HR manager dealt with the situation. The manager told me that David was asked to leave, but argued that he had to do his job. He was eventually escorted out by security.

Over the course of the next few days David was seen by members of staff hanging around the streets outside the store all day, but nobody investigated why.

John Ridge, who was the HR director for all Lewis's stores and who had once been the HR manager of the Manchester store, heard of this situation from one of the HR assistants and came by train from London. John was a great character. In his lifetime, he had been a Major in the British Army and led a regiment of the Gurkhas in Nepal. He was a brave man who commanded a lot of admiration from the staff and respect from his superiors because of the values he held. He came to the Manchester store and asked me to describe the details of what had happened and what we at the store had done to help David. He listened intently to my version of events. His questions were not focused on why we had let David go, but on what we had done to help him with this current crisis.

I had to admit I had not done a lot.

John then asked where David was and was told he usually could be found somewhere outside the store. He left the store to find David and eventually returned with him and asked me to join them in the HR office. John asked David several questions and found out that the reason he had been coming to the store every day was

*that he could not bear to tell his wife he had lost his job
because he was frightened of the affect it would have
on her. He explained he had always done this job and
his family was dependent on the income and stability
of it. He described that he knew nothing else and was
immensely frightened about the future and the impact
the job loss would have on him personally. "What will I
do all day?" he asked.*

*John was honest, he told David the reasons why the
job had to go, and that he could not change that, but he
persuaded David to agree on an action plan to try and
find alternative solutions. John went home with David
to explain to his wife what had happened and why. He
charged the HR personnel to help David find another job
and soon thereafter David found a position in another
store in the area. He asked me to arrange dinner with
David and his friends and family as a farewell gesture
from the company.*

*This incident was personally mortifying and
embarrassing for me, but had a great bearing on my own
values and the way I have tried to act as a manager since*

then. John taught me the value of being open and honest, treating others with dignity, being supportive, getting personally involved in specific situations, and the simple power of listening.

Watching him asking questions of David in that office— and hearing him out—and the positive affect it had on the crisis, has helped me to never act boldly or rashly without listening again.

How well do you listen? Do you concentrate on what others are saying or are you busy thinking about what you want to say next? Do you believe others have something to teach you? What can you do to improve as a listener?

Listen. Listening is one of those dynamics that sounds like the easiest thing in the world to do, but in reality is one of the hardest.

The mind of a person with understanding gets knowledge; the wise person listens to learn more.

PROVERBS 18:15 NCV

PRAYING

Prayer may not change things for you,
but it for sure changes you for things.

—SAMUEL M. SHOEMAKER

Walking through a crowded airport, I saw a man kneeling reverently on a beautiful prayer rug, his head touching the ground, his body pointing toward the east. I was visibly reminded that all of the great faith traditions of the world affirm our need to pray. The man's dedicated prayer convicted me of my own need to pray.

As a Christian, I draw great comfort and hope from Jesus' words that, though He is physically removed from us, the Heavenly Father has given the Holy Spirit to live within us and advocate for us here on Earth (John 14:15-17). Jesus goes on to say that the Spirit is our "teacher" (John 14:26-27). Do you ever think of God as your teacher? Think of the greatest teacher you have ever learned from in your life. How much more must God have to teach us?

I do believe that we are enriched spiritually and mentally—even physically—through an active prayer life. Yes, when we pray, God acts on our behalf in the world. But I think it is more often the case that the greatest change is within us.

If prayer truly is conversation with a real, living, personal, listening, speaking God—and I believe it is— then prayer is not a one-way street. I have learned that one of the biggest needs we have in prayer is learning to listen more. That can be a struggle for me. I feel like I know how to tell God I love Him and I need him. But I don't feel as good at being silent and waiting to hear what He has to say to me. I suspect I'm not alone.

Some things that might help you and me include:

- Fill your mind with God's thoughts by reading your Bible as part of your prayer time.
- Reaffirm your belief that we are in relationship with God, and that He speaks to us today.

- Take time to be silent—something that's oh so tough in our noise- and media-saturated society—and listen to God.
- Maintain receptiveness to God's whispers throughout the day so that you grasp the unique and creative ways God wants to speak to you.

If you want to grow through a lifestyle of learning, there is no better source of wisdom than God, all-wise and all-knowing. Just remember, prayer with God should be a conversation. Don't just come before Him with a list of needs and a bunch of words. Take time to listen. After all, one of the key ways we learn is through listening. Who better to listen to than God?

Rejoice always, pray without ceasing, in everything give thanks; for this is the will of God in Christ Jesus for you.
1 THESSALONIANS 5:16-18 NKJV

UNLEARNING

The illiterate of the 21st century will not be
those who cannot read and write,
but those who cannot learn, unlearn, and relearn.

—ALVIN TOFFLER

The old adage teaches us that practice makes perfect. But what if we practice doing things the wrong way? You can go through three or four buckets of tennis balls every day to improve your serve, but what if you were taught wrong technique from your first instructor?

There are two problems with all that we have learned in the past. We might have gotten it wrong the first time. But even if we did learn what worked in the past, the world is changing rapidly. So, the old ways may no longer be the right ways.

When we introduced computer technology at Walmart, our biggest challenge was not finding the hardware or programming the software to dramatically improve our operations. Our challenge was introducing new technology to people at every level of the company who were already very comfortable with how we were doing things at the present. We quickly discovered that in order to introduce major change, we not only needed to budget learning time, but also unlearning time.

I'm not one who needs major change in the air to be happy. I have seen that when management constantly creates a state of flux and change, it is destabilizing and hurts morale. All of us, however, need to be ready to embrace positive changes. And when those times come, they often bring the difficult and painful task of cutting off previous ways of thinking and doing things.

There is one thing we never have to worry about. God doesn't change. And though certainly not as reliable as God, well thought-through beliefs and values don't change either. Just about everything else in life is up for grabs—work processes and systems, fashion, communication methods, and other derivatives.

For you to go to the next level in your thinking, what do you need to let go of or unlearn? Peter Drucker argues that the first step in managing change is *organized abandonment*. When you are unlearning, note the things that do not require change. Even if you haven't defined your values, you still have them. They are only buried. This unlearning exercise may be one way for you to discover your values. At The Soderquist Center, we believe leadership is at its best when it is grounded in sound and refined values. They guard us from constantly unlearning. There are some things that don't change.

Why is change so hard? How open to change are you? In a world of change, some things don't.

Behold, I will do a new thing, now it shall spring forth; Shall you not know it? I will even make a road in the wilderness and rivers in the desert.

ISAIAH 43:19 NKJV

HEARING GREAT SPEAKERS

The wisdom of the wise and the experience of the ages are perpetuated by quotations.

—BENJAMIN D. ISRAELI

From time to time, we would invite an outside speaker to our Saturday managers' meetings at Walmart to share their story and leadership principles with us. I found that even if their comments reinforced the existing Walmart principles we already knew, they had a powerful ability to refresh our understanding. Sometimes, the things that we tried teaching ourselves at Walmart just didn't stick until we heard it from someone outside the company.

It was helpful to hear other people as diverse as investor Warren Buffet and baseball legend Hank Aaron. More recently, Walmart has hosted Facebook founder Mark Zuckerberg and IBM CEO Ginni

Rometty. These outside voices brought fresh ideas on leadership and reinforce methods we were already using. Being able to hear influential people and great speakers was important in keeping our team motivated and in an attitude of learning.

But you don't have to be a manager at Walmart to hear great speakers. Today, there are more chances than ever to access groundbreaking ideas and lasting wisdom.

- TED Talks
- Lecture series at universities
- Leadership seminars
- Civic organizations
- Chamber of Commerce meetings
- Special speakers in local churches

Just type the name of a great leader into the search window of YouTube and you will be amazed at what is available—including speeches from Roosevelt and Churchill to a host of other greats who were alive during the advent of still and motion photography.

If you are in or near a university city, stretch yourself and go listen to academic thoughts that (a) you might not agree with and (b) that may require a lot more brainpower to understand (or partially understand) than you are used to expending.

Like physical exercise, sometimes we need to push our mental abilities to keep intellectually toned and vigorous.

Are you actively looking for opportunities to learn? When was the last time you carved out time to hear someone with great ideas speak? Many people note that learning is like exercising a muscle. Reading, listening to the radio, or watching a TED Talk online, especially after concentrating for a full day at work, expands your ability to learn and your aptitude for success. Are you taking advantage of opportunities to learn around you?

Listen to counsel and receive instruction,
that you may be wise in your latter days.

PROVERBS 19:20 NKJV

FINDING GREAT ROLE MODELS

The most important single influence in the life of a person is another person who is worthy of emulation.

—PAUL D. SHAFER

Most of us look up to and respect certain people in our lives. For some, it may be a parent or family member. For others, it may be a teacher, a youth leader, or pastor. For even others, it may be a celebrity—a sports hero, an actor, or a singer. We admire these people because of their talent, the way they look, the way they do their job, the way they dress, or how they make us feel. We like them so much that sometimes we dress or act or talk like them. These people are our role models.

As you were growing up, who did you admire? Who do you aspire to be more like now? I think it is healthy to have role models. Good ones can provide standards for us, and can inspire us to be the best we can be–to achieve more than we would have on our own.

Because a role model can be an enormous influence on how we think and act, it is critical that we choose these people with great care. It is very possible—and we see examples of it almost every day—to pick someone who could influence us negatively and move us to do wrong.

I was blessed to work directly with several great leaders. Sam Walton and David Glass were incredible leaders. I benefited immeasurably from just watching them lead. They were both bright, passionate and full of energy. They enjoyed life and treated everyone with respect and dignity. While they were different, they both got results and they each had a tremendous influence on my own leadership.

What is hard to illustrate, however, is how much people whose names you wouldn't recognize have influenced me. The influence of all those people—those who aren't famous by our standards—in my life has far exceeded what I might have ever expected. We should always be alert to what we can learn from others. Ultimately, this means that we have to be consciously aware of what we see in them to determine how that may positively impact our lives.

I received a note in the mail a number of years ago while still working at Walmart that underscored this truth.

The first time someone asked, "Remember the lady who was always so friendly at the door of Walmart?" her face jumped immediately to my mind. It soon became apparent that this was not an isolated experience— more than a few people knew this woman as the friendly face at the door of Walmart.

In those first days after her death, no one seemed to know what her name was. But she had touched people and they remembered her. What a wonderful tribute to a lady who smiled, said hello, and asked if we needed a cart.

The lesson for us is that our actions, no matter how small, whether positive or negative, private or public, will impact others, perhaps far more than we ever imagine. This lady realized the power of that connectedness and utilized it. With smiles, words, and small gestures she was, in a few moments of contact, able to touch people.

If only we all could be remembered with such fondness by strangers who did not even know our name.

Wow! Talk about a powerful testimony. I can tell you that anonymous woman not only touched the lives of hundreds who met her at the front door of that Walmart store, but my life as well. From the day that Doris Sutterer jotted these lines to me, I have made a conscious effort to smile, say hello, and be helpful to everyone around me.

Certainly the ultimate role model for us to follow is Jesus Christ. The term "Christian" literally means "Christ like." And as we grow and mature spiritually, our very image—how we think and act—should be changing to look more and more like His.

Who is your role model? Are your eyes open, finding other role models that will inspire you to grow and learn?

Imitate me, just as I also imitate Christ.

1 CORINTHIANS 11:1 NKJV

READING GREAT BOOKS

You are the same today that you are going to be five years from now except for two things: the people with whom you associate and the books you read.

—CHARLES "TREMENDOUS" JONES

A recent study by the Pew Institute revealed:

- 33% of high school graduates never read another book the rest of their lives.
- 42% of college graduates never read another book after college.
- 57% of new books are not read to completion.
- 70% of US adults have not been in a bookstore in the last five years.
- 80% of US families did not buy or read a book last year.

All I can say is "Wow!" It makes me wonder who in the world is reading all the new books being published each year. And it makes me want to say thank you—and kudos to you—for reading this book. Could it be that when it comes to acquiring new knowledge, the rich are getting richer and the poor are getting poorer?

I've read—and whether or not it is exactly true I still believe it in essence—that reading one hour a day in your chosen field will make you an international expert in seven years.

I have found reading to be valuable in my own life. Of course, the fact that you are holding a book in your hands right now means that you share at least some of my sentiments on the topic. But if you need a good reason to continue making reading a part of your daily routine, here are four benefits to the practice:

Mental Exercise—When you watch television, you don't have to engage your imagination or the full range of thought processes required with reading. Maybe that's why so many choose not to read; it's a little harder. But just as physical exercise makes you stronger, reading makes you mentally sharper.

Deeper Levels of Thinking—We gather so much of our understanding of the world through TV and the internet. Yet, the material is often presented with brevity in the form of attention-grabbing sound bites, not in-depth coverage. Books and other forms of print media can go much deeper into a topic. As you read about important subjects, they will better challenge your thinking and grow you intellectually.

More Interesting Conversation—No one likes an intellectual snob or showoff, but as a rule, you become a more interesting conversationalist when you read.

Spiritual Development—When Gutenberg invented the printing press to produce the Bible for the common man, he forever linked the printed word with spiritual growth.

There are great books to choose from in every category of interest you have—political science, history, mystery and adventure, Christian living, humor, and technical subjects. Pick areas that are positive. When you read a novel, can you find principles for living? What do we learn from the past? Read what you like—and push yourself to grow by trying new areas.

Of course, reading is an excellent way to learn about leadership. During my time at Walmart, I encouraged all of our management associates to buy really good books on leadership and start their own library. To encourage them, I would purchase thousands of a particular book and pass one out to every manager who attended the year beginning meetings. Let me challenge you to establish your own library of great books and set goals for reading. They don't have to be all about leadership, but just good books. Think about the reading habits you had in your school days. Underlining, highlighting, and writing in the text can help you absorb more as you read.

Finally, all this reading shouldn't edge out God's Word. David, one of the greatest leaders in all of history, said when praying to God, "When I remember You on my bed, I meditate on You in the night watches" (Psalm 63:6 NKJV). What a good way to start and end your day.

I recently bought a new computer. In order to set it up correctly, I had to carefully consult the instruction packet that came with the computer. After I got it set up, I didn't know how to use it until I read more of the instruction manual. I still have to look up how to use certain functions. I couldn't live my spiritual life without the ultimate instruction manual for life, the Bible. The Bible showed me how to get started, showed me where my source of power was and how to stay connected to that power.

There are many stories in the Bible that have illustrated for me the things I should and should not do. I could never have operated my computer without reading the instruction manual, and I could never live the spiritual life without consistently reading the Bible.

So what book is on your nightstand? Or on your tablet? Leaders are readers!

...The judgments of the Lord are true; they are completely right. They are worth more than gold, even the purest gold. They are sweeter than honey, even the finest honey.

PSALMS 19:9-10 NCV

BEING WILLING TO CHANGE

The key to change is first to understand what not to change and then to feel free to change everything else.
A key factor to Walmart's trajectory is that it has never changed its DNA. Central to this set of core traits is a fanatical adherence to a deeply democratic idea...

—JIM COLLINS

Change is hard. Let me put that differently—change is very hard!

Change may be one of the hardest things we do. But it is essential that we maintain an open mind and heart or we will miss out on achieving our full potential. That doesn't mean that we should change for change's sake. That drives everyone around us crazy and really doesn't accomplish anything. Senseless change breeds a lack of commitment to new programs and distrust in leadership.

There needs to be a real purpose behind every change we make, and we do need to curb our natural tendency to do things the same way we always have. It is in our willingness to change that we discover new and better ways to live, learn, and lead.

I was at a banquet one evening and had the opportunity to visit with Harry Cunningham, the former CEO of K-Mart stores. He was the legendary character who dramatically changed retail in America by developing the concept of the K-Mart store for the former Kresge Company. I thanked him for what he had done in pioneering the successful discounting format as we know it today. He was very gracious in accepting my praise, but was quick to add how much he appreciated what Walmart had done in developing the concept even further.

He went on to say, "We made a serious mistake along the way by not changing and updating our stores over the years. We had a successful formula that was working and saw no reason to change. You folks at Walmart continued to improve until you were much better than we were, and by that time, you passed us by."

The lesson for me in that conversation was that while success can lead to greater success, it could also lead to failure if you refuse to focus on improving.

In Walmart, we had what we called a low "RC factor"—that is, a low Resistance to Change. Over time we continued to change—and hopefully improve—just about everything we did and how we did it. Sam built a team that was obsessed with better meeting the needs of customers through better stores, better prices, and better service.

I've talked about the importance of values. The truth is, they were the foundation of that low RC factor and our culture. We refused to change our values. The core beliefs we had about treating people fairly, telling the truth, being honest in our dealings with everyone, keeping promises, and striving for excellence formed the foundation of how we interacted with everyone inside and outside the company, including our customers. Somehow at Walmart, we were able to find a good balance between changing things that didn't work and standing on a firm foundation while doing it.

Are you open to change? Do you have a low RC factor? Do you have timeless values that help you know what areas of your life should never be changed?

....

He who keeps instruction is in the way of life,
but he who refuses correction goes astray.

PROVERBS 10:17 NKJV

....

FOLLOWING A GUIDE

Trust the Lord with all your and lean not to your own understanding. In all your ways acknowledge Him and He will direct your path.

PROVERBS 3:5-6 NKJV

Many years ago, when our son was a missionary in the Indian sub-continent, my wife and youngest son and I flew over to meet him and see what he was doing. We met him first in Nepal and spent a week traveling around Kathmandu and the surrounding area. He pointed out many interesting sites, introduced us to his co-workers and shared with us the work he was doing. We saw more and learned more in a short week than we ever could have on our own because our son had lived there and knew his way around.

We then flew to New Delhi, India. Although our son had lived in other parts of India, he had not traveled in some of the areas we wanted to see. We decided to hire a guide to drive us around. Our guide had lived in India all of his life and had been recommended to us by someone else who had used him before. He knew the best sites to see, the best way to get there, and the history of every place we visited.

We toured the capital city of New Delhi and on to Agra where we were awestruck by the magnificent Taj Mahal, one of the New Seven Wonders of the World. We traveled to Jaipur a city where all of the centuries-old buildings were pink in color and had been the home of many of the Maharajas who had lived in these grand palaces. It wasn't just the destinations that made our trip so rich; it was the journey itself.

As we drove through the countryside and little villages, we got a wonderful taste of everyday life in India: the farmers tilling their fields with oxen, the ladies weaving beautiful rugs and colorful shawls, the shop keepers in their small stores selling the basics of life, the beautiful scenery along the road ways and the wonderful people of India. We knew we would never have accomplished so much if we had tried to do it alone.

We recognized that we would probably be in India only one time in our lives and therefore we wanted to see and learn as much as we possibly could. In reflection, I realize that it was even more than what we saw and learned, it was what we experienced. It was also the memories that we still have which have enriched our lives.

We only have one life to live and will never go around again. There is so much more we can see and do. Do you want to see and learn as much as you can in your lifetime? Do you want to experience life to the fullest? One way to do it is to select the best guide you can find, someone who has been there before—particularly in unfamiliar circumstances and life transitions. It is so important to pick the right guide. If you don't, you could end up going in the wrong direction and missing important and exciting opportunities along the way. In India, we chose the right guide.

If you're interested, I know a guide that I can recommend to you. He has been our guide for many years. Our children have followed Him and they in turn have introduced Him to all of our grandchildren. He is always there and has never let any of us down. From time to time, we have gone out on our own but fortunately we have come back because we got lost without Him.

Let me introduce you to our family guide: His name is Jesus. He came into this world as a baby and lived a simple life healing the sick and doing good. He paid the ultimate price by giving His life as a sacrifice for our sins; yours and mine. He has shown us the keys to an abundant life in Him. We can actually know the Almighty God in a personal way and seek Him to guide our lives day by day. All we need to do is accept the gift of His Son's life and sacrifice and receive Jesus into our lives as Lord and Savior.

Show me Your ways, O Lord;
teach me Your paths.
Lead me in Your truth and teach me,
for You are the God of my salvation;
on You I wait all the day.

PSALMS 25:4-5 NKJV

ONE SOLITARY LIFE

He was born in an obscure village,
a child of a peasant woman.

He grew up in another obscure village where
he worked in a carpenter shop until he was 30.
Then for three years he was an itinerant preacher.

He never had a family. Or owned a home.
He never set foot inside a big city. He never traveled
two hundred miles from the place he was born.

He never wrote a book or held an office.
He did none of the things that usually accompany greatness.

While he was still a young man,
the tide of popular opinion turned against him.

His friends deserted him.
He was turned over to his enemies.

He went through the mockery of a trial.
He was nailed to a cross between two thieves.

While he was dying his executioners gambled
for the only piece of property he had, his coat.

When he was dead, he was taken down
and laid in a borrowed grave.

Nineteen centuries have come and gone and today he is
still the central figure for much of the human race.

All the armies that ever marched, all the navies that ever
sailed, and all the parliaments that ever sat, and all the kings
that ever reigned, put together have not affect the life of man
upon this earth as powerfully as this One Solitary Life.

—JAMES ALLAN FRANCIS

PART 3

LEAD TO MAKE A DIFFERENCE

I will send you to Pharaoh that you may bring My people,
the children of Israel, out of Egypt.

EXODUS 3:10 NKJV

Leadership is about taking an organization to
a place it would not have otherwise gone without you,
in a value-adding, measurable way.

—GEORGE M.C. FISHER

Every great institution is the lengthened shadow
of a single man. His character determines
the character of his organization.

—RALPH WALDO EMERSON

PUTTING YOUR VALUES FIRST

Good values are easier caught than taught.

—ZIG ZIGLAR

When I first joined Walmart, wherever I spoke, people wanted to know how Walmart had managed to be so successful though we were still quite a small company compared to the giant retailers of those days. I usually shared from a list of Walmart strategies, including our real estate strategy, our everyday low pricing, our merchandise assortment, our people programs, and numerous other business strategies. After a while, I began to realize that these strategies weren't the ultimate root of our success. For one thing, we certainly weren't the only company with good business practices. And I came to realize that, to be effective, we had to constantly fine-tune our strategies. But there was something much more fundamental that didn't change: the foundational beliefs and values of the company. It became apparent to me that everything we did grew out of our beliefs, our values.

In what is probably too cynical—but also, too often true—of a statement, J. Ian Morrison says, "Most organizations have values written by the marketing department, spoken by the CEO, and espoused by no one else in the organization." But because of Sam Walton's relentless passion to instill certain values into his company—and I promise you, he talked and practiced his values from morning to night every single day—if you stop any associate in Walmart and ask them what our three basic beliefs are, you will hear the following in their own words:

- We treat everyone with respect and dignity.
- We are in business to satisfy our customers.
- We strive for excellence in all that we do.

Now when I speak or am interviewed about the secrets of Walmart's success, I begin with values. I have had many people suggest that all this talk about values sounds more like a comforting bromide—mom, apple pie, and baseball—rather than like secrets to success. Our values and beliefs are simple. There is no question about that. But Walmart people understand what the company values mean and work hard to make them a reality every day. It's not just what's written in the handbook or posted on the walls—not just dreamed up by the marketing department. To work, our values must be lived out on every level in our personal lives at home and professional lives inside our companies.

I've come to realize that beliefs and values together determine how a company operates and whether it reaches its full potential.

I have seen companies that have shady practices thrive for a period of time. But the success never lasts. Whether it is a scandal or a long-term erosion of customer loyalty, doing business—doing life—without values is shortsighted and leads to failure.

I'm not going to mention it by name, but there's a privately held, family owned company—a highly successful and industry leading company—in a nearby state that I've always had the utmost respect for. From a distance I've admired the way they do business and serve their customers. It was like a punch in the stomach when I heard that the FBI had raided their corporate offices after a number of their corporate customers—most were small to medium-sized business owners—reported that they were being cheated out of substantial financial promises. As I write these words, the investigation is ongoing and no indictments have been made. But with huge financial settlements already being made, and with a number of the company's key senior executives agreeing to cooperate with the investigation in exchange for immunity from prosecution, I suspect that a company with a history of operating with high values just might have lost its way, cut some corners, and decided improved margins were more important than maintaining the founder's way of doing business.

I hope I'm wrong. But whatever the case here, there are just too many stories of companies that do unbelievable damage to countless others—and to themselves—when their executives stop leading with values.

Values are essential in business and the same is true on an individual level. Will I lie to a customer or ask someone who works for me to do something unethical? That depends on whether I value other people over my own success. Will I fudge a little on my taxes? That depends on my beliefs about obeying the laws and doing what I consider right. Will I flirt around with colleagues at work as long as I can claim it is harmless? That depends on how much I value my marriage.

Values matter in everything we do. What do your values look like in everyday life? Do they change with your circumstance?

And by the way, have you written your values down yet? Your values are that core set of principles you will live by no matter where you work, no matter what your position, no matter who else is watching.

Blessed is the man who walks not in the counsel of the ungodly, nor stands in the path of sinners, nor sits in the seat of the scornful; but his delight is in the law of the Lord, and in His law he meditates day and night.

PSALMS 1:1-2 NKJV

BEING PASSIONATE

....

A platoon leader doesn't get his platoon to go by getting up and shouting, "I am smarter. I am bigger. I am stronger. I am the leader." He gets men to go along with him because they want to do it for him and they believe in him.

—DWIGHT D. EISENHOWER
....

There have been a lot of books written about leadership—good books with many valid suggestions. I appreciate the simplicity of what Daniel Goleman says: "Great leaders move us. They ignite our passion and inspire the best in us."

That's what leaders do. They move us to do something that we wouldn't think, or have the faith, to do on our own. They light the spark that causes us to get excited and pour our whole selves into a noble work. They are the encourager who makes us strive for excellence and become the best we can be.

Leaders are the motivating force behind every major accomplishment—good and bad—the world has ever known. Consider World War II. Hitler incited the masses to destroy the shops of innocent Jews, burn books, and far worse through his public oratory. On the other hand, Churchill, in his nightly radio broadcasts, rallied the English people in their "darkest hour" to never surrender. In the minds of their followers, both men painted pictures of something powerful all could be a part of. How did both of these men rally people so effectively? They were passionate.

We have all listened to leaders who are very intelligent and can clearly see things that we don't, but lack an ability to transfer that picture into our minds. It's probably not because they can't communicate their vision. Oftentimes, the problem is that the vision they are attempting to articulate doesn't come from the heart, and we easily sense that. As a result, we aren't moved to make the vision a reality. For passion to be contagious, it must begin in your heart.

When we lead others, whether at work, in church, in educational settings, or in our families, our objective needs to be to gain commitment to the work at hand. People who are only complying with your requests or rules and regulations will, at best, do only what you ask them to do. People who are committed to your vision, on the other hand, will not only do what you ask, but go far beyond and do all that they possibly can to accomplish the goal.

We had a store manager who had a special passion for helping people grow their potential. In his store in Manhattan, Kansas, a university town in which a lot of our associates were college students, he trained more young people for assistant and store manager positions than I believe anyone else in all of Walmart. His leadership style fostered a desire in young people to move forward and excel. He was instrumental in helping students take off in significant careers with Walmart and other companies. It wasn't his position that enabled him to impact so many young leaders in Walmart. It was his passion.

Do people follow you because of your position or title? Or do they follow you because they believe in you? Because they are committed to your leadership and desire to follow? Do you move people, ignite their passion, and inspire them to be the best that they can be?

....

And whatever you do, do it heartily, as to the Lord and
not to men, knowing that from the Lord you will receive
the reward of the inheritance; for you serve the Lord Christ.

COLOSSIANS 3:23-24 NKJV

....

CREATING TEAMWORK

*The most important measure of how good a game I played
was how much better I'd made my teammates play.*

—BILL RUSSELL

I love sports. I love the excitement of competition and the feeling of accomplishment when I have given my very best— win or lose. Of course, now, giving my very best usually means cheering enthusiastically for the basketball team my son coaches at John Brown University or for my grandchildren when they play soccer, basketball, or other sports.

There are great lessons to apply to life and leadership from sports. One of the most important ones is the power of teamwork. It isn't necessarily the team with the most superstars or highest payroll that wins the Super Bowl or World Series. A great team will often beat a group of highly talented individuals because the true team has learned to play together.

Phil Jackson is widely considered one of the greatest professional basketball coaches of all time. He won eleven NBA championships in his career; six with the Chicago Bulls and Michael Jordan and five with Kobe Bryant and the Los Angeles Lakers. In his book, *11 Rings,* Jackson contrasts the leadership abilities of the two players. "One of the biggest differences between the two stars from my perspective was Michael's superior skills as a leader." Jackson continued, "Though at times he could be hard on his teammates, Michael was masterful at controlling the emotional climate of the team with the power of his presence. Kobe had a long way to go before he could make that claim."

One apparent distinction was how they related to their teammates. "[Michael] loved hanging out with his teammates and security guards, playing cards, smoking cigars, and joking around," Jackson said in the book. He couldn't say the same for Kobe.

As a young professional, Michael Jordan led the NBA in scoring for four of his first six seasons. One season, he averaged over thirty-seven points per game.

Still, the Bulls team had a losing season that year (40-42 in 1986-87). They never won a championship during that first six-year span with Jordan. But the Bulls' ownership group kept adding key players—not superstars but role players—to the roster. Some people called those great Bulls teams of the nineties a rag-tag collection of players and personalities, but each player knew what he had to offer. Soon, the team's winning became more important than individual success. Michael Jordan never again averaged as many points as he did early in his career, but the Chicago Bulls won six NBA championships.

A more contemporary example is LeBron James. There is no doubt he could average more points than he does. With his combination of size, quickness, and skill, he is almost unstoppable. But he is known as one of the most unselfish players in the league. He is not only a gifted scorer but also a gifted passer. Why? He knows you don't win championships without teamwork.

A generation ago, enhanced teamwork created an incredible turnaround for the Bulls and became the true measure of Jordan's basketball greatness. The same happened in recent years for LeBron and the Miami Heat.

Is the power of teamwork true just of sports? Absolutely not! I've seen it work over and over again in all walks of life. Sam Walton was a wonderful leader, but he had an incredible company behind him the whole time. Walmart is a great example of ordinary people working together as a team and achieving something extraordinary. Of course there were plenty of talented individuals, but what was most remarkable was the teamwork.

One of the key words in business today is collaboration. It is not necessarily a warm and fuzzy word as it is usually applied to productivity tools. But it's still about teamwork. How can we leverage technology and platforms to make it easier for our people to work well together?

In 1 Corinthians, Paul says that we are all one body made up of many parts. We need every part in order for the body to function properly. We can't all be arms or eyes or feet. We are made differently and therefore complement each other by design. No one person has all the answers or can do it all. We accomplish much more if we know our own abilities, recognize that other people do some things better than we do, and encourage others to contribute their strengths, too.

Are you a team player? Could you accomplish more if you worked more closely with others? And why shouldn't we work alongside others, getting and giving help as needed? Fine-tuned teamwork is the quickest route to maximizing a group's potential.

...We are many, but in Christ we are all one body.
Each one is a part of that body,
and each part belongs to all the other parts.

ROMANS 12:5 NCV

TREATING EVERYONE WITH RESPECT

Life is made up, not of great sacrifice or duties,
but of little things, in which smiles and kindness
and small obligations win and preserve the heart.

—HUMPHREY DAVY

I was traveling around to Walmart stores one day and stopped in a smaller store that had been open thirteen or fourteen years. While it looked a little dated and was very crowded, it was clear that the store was operated well and that the associates were doing a good job of keeping the store neat, clean, and well stocked.

After walking through and looking to see if I could offer any assistance, I met with a group of associates in the lunchroom. I told them I thought they were doing a great job of keeping the store attractive and taking care of our customers. They were emphatic about how well their manager treated them and, without any prompting, went on to add how much he cared about them as individuals. Many of the associates said that he was the best manager they ever had.

I asked them how they knew he cared for them. One of the ladies shared a simple story with the group. She said that several years before, when there was a different manager, her daughter was being inducted into the National Honor Society. The school was holding a special recognition ceremony the next evening for the students and their parents, and she was scheduled to work. When she had gone to that manager and explained the situation, it was obvious that he was unhappy. He gave her a rough time about it and said that she would have to find someone to take her place for the evening. He further told her to never let it happen again. She did find another associate to work for her and ended up going to the school program. But on a night that should have been filled with joy over her daughter's accomplishment, she felt guilty and worried the whole time—like she had done something wrong.

She went on to say that she recently had a similar situation. Her youngest son had been selected to play in a Little League All-Star game on a day when she had been scheduled to work. She went to the current manager and explained the situation. He let her know that he thought that her son's accomplishment was wonderful and that she must be a proud mother. She quickly offered to find someone to take her place. He declined saying that he would take care of it himself. She went to the game and thoroughly enjoyed the evening. The following day, the manager made a beeline to her and asked how the game went and how her son played.

In both cases, this woman attended her children's activities. In the first case, she felt horrible. In the second case, she felt great. It was all in how her manager responded to what most of us would consider to be a very reasonable request.

This example impressed on me again how we can impact other people's feelings—both for the good and for the bad—through the way we respect and treat them.

Everyone I know wants to be treated fairly, to feel that people respect them and genuinely care about them. It's easy to say that we respect other people, but sometimes our actions don't back up our talk. Those in leadership positions should always show respect for everyone—but especially the people who work for them.

When you demonstrate to people that you care about them, they will be much more inclined to follow you.

Interest. Attention. Fairness. Kindness. Concern. Encouragement.

Do you offer such attitudes and actions to everyone you work with, whether they are new to the company or a senior executive? Or do you offer such respect only to those who you think can help you?

How you treat everyone you encounter is the measure of the genuineness of your respect—and the heights you can reach as a leader.

When you do things, do not let selfishness
or pride be your guide. Instead, be humble and give
more honor to others than to yourselves.

PHILIPPIANS 2:3 NCV

LEAD TO MAKE A DIFFERENCE BY...

SPENDING TIME WITH PEOPLE

Most leaders spend time trying to get others
to think highly of them, when instead they should try
to get their people to think more highly of themselves.
It's wonderful when the people believe in their leader.
It's more wonderful when the leader believes in their people!

—BOOKER T. WASHINGTON

There's a popular and Emmy Award winning TV show on CBS called Undercover Boss. The premise is very simple. Company CEOs or other top managers go incognito to work in the trenches with their employees to see what their work life is really like. The goal is to see ways they can improve work conditions.

One of the best US episodes is still the first show when Larry O'Donnell, the President and CEO of Waste Management, hopped aboard one of the trucks and got a taste for what his workers did each day. I thought that was very brave and noble of him. What a great idea.

You don't have to be selected for an episode of Undercover Boss to get close to your people. I believe one of the keys to Walmart's incredible growth and success was Sam's commitment to that principle. I give examples of that throughout this book. Sam believed in being with his people at every level of the company. It permeated our culture.

You've heard of the concept Management By Walking Around, or MBWA. Sam would have added an 'L' to that acronym: Listening. He practiced Management By Walking Around and Listening. In fact, he routinely modeled that at the Home Office and out in stores visiting with associates. He made a habit of actively listening to cashiers and hourly associates.

Another behavior Sam consistently demonstrated was quick and frequent visits with new officers, especially when they were promoted early in their careers. He was known to show up unannounced in their offices during the first week on their job. And, as they jumped up to greet him at the door, Sam would often maneuver around the office desk until he was standing behind the desk chair while the bewildered vice president stood by the door. As the young officer wondered what had just happened, Sam would slam the palm of his hand on the back of the chair and say, "Let me tell you something that I don't ever want you to forget. Never make a crucial decision sitting in this chair."

In my years with Walmart I was witness to many significant management decisions that were altered because that truth was instilled in our leadership early and often. I remember a particular story of a new regional vice president who received a phone call from a district manager relaying information about a store manager he was about to fire due to underperformance.

With Sam's hand-slapping experience fresh in this young leader's mind, he responded, "Hold on, I'll fly out on Monday. I'd like to find out more about this situation." That Monday morning, after walking the store and talking with many of the associates, he found out that the store manger's wife had been recently diagnosed with cancer and he was really struggling personally. This store manager was trying to help his wife all he could, take care of their two children, and run the store. This was creating immense pressure and he was under a great deal of personal stress. The vice president decided to visit with the district manager and scheduled a lunch meeting. He immediately began to ask him a series of questions.

"I can see that the manager is struggling. Do you know what the real problem is?"

"When did you first notice the decline in performance?"

"Do you know the name of the manager's wife?"

"How is she doing? Have you asked anyone?"

"How many times do you stop by the store each week?"

What this young officer had discovered in one morning of walking around and talking with the store associates was that they loved the manager and that he had been a good and consistent leader. His wife's illness had changed everything. It was obvious that, while the district manager was correct about the store, he had only looked at the numbers and failed to find out the real cause. Our young vice president told him that he had two choices. "You can leave the company immediately or go back to the store and make things right."

Upon returning to the store, the regional vice president gathered and addressed all the associates, "We need you to rally around your manager. As you have told me, he's struggling with significant family issues. We are going to give him as much time as he needs with his family while we appoint an interim manager. Let's all pitch in so when he returns he will be proud of his Walmart family and will come back to a store that's thriving."

Ultimately, the store manager was able to return full-time to his position and served in that capacity for many years in a very successful store. Equally as important, the Monday trip became a defining moment in both the district manager's and young regional vice president's careers.

It's not always convenient to drop what you are working on and go to where there may be problems. It may seem like a waste of time to stop and visit with people as you walk up and down the aisles. But, let me tell you, it's a big deal to them. At Walmart, we worked hard at finding ways to make it an important part of a leader's job expectations.

As any organization grows, it becomes harder and harder to keep in touch with all of the people. At one time, Sam visited every store at least once a year. The associates loved it when he would stop by their store. He talked to everyone he saw, especially the hourly associates. He made them feel comfortable to say whatever was on their minds.

As we grew, Sam insisted that all the senior officers travel to the stores at least once a week. He encouraged all home office associates, especially buyers, to visit stores and talk with as many associates as possible, listen to what they had to say, and learn from them. Those visits really served several purposes. First, it was important to see how the stores looked and how well we were serving the customers. But it was also important for the store associates to see and visit with the leaders of the company and to recognize that, in every respect, they were just normal people like themselves. It helped everyone work more closely with each other and helped to build trust between associates in the field and those back at the home office. We learned a lot about how we could be more effective and correct mistakes we were making.

If you really believe that your people are important to your success, you are right, because they are. If you really want to encourage your people to do their best, they must trust you. They can only trust you if they get to know you. If you believe that is true, you will find a way, in your busy schedule, to reach out to people and let them see who you really are and that you care about them.

I don't know who may be reading this book, but let me encourage you to really learn to respect other people. Learn to listen. I don't care if it's work, home, community, school, church or wherever else you interact. We are all in the "people business." Don't make important judgments sitting behind your desk.

And when Jesus went out He saw a great multitude; and He was moved with compassion for them, and healed their sick.

MATTHEW 14:14 NKJV

ACTING WITH INTEGRITY

Character is doing the right thing when nobody's looking.
There are too many people who think that
the only thing that's right is to get by,
and the only thing that's wrong is to get caught.

—J.C. WATTS

Leaders demonstrate integrity and character by their actions and their words. They keep their promises. They demonstrate by their behavior the true depth of their beliefs—and it aligns with what they say. When you watch and listen to them, they make you feel like you want to be better yourself. Have you had a leader like that in your life? Maybe a parent or teacher or community volunteer?

Once, I got an envelope on my desk from an officer in the company with a note that said,

"Use this if you want. If not, just toss it."

I looked inside and there was a series of profit and loss statements for a competitor of ours. Wow! What a treasure trove. I had heard of companies paying a lot of money to get valuable information like this—a practice often referred to as corporate espionage. And here it was on my desk, free of charge. Those numbers could have put us at an advantage over that competitor, but I tossed the report in the trash. It wasn't my property; it belonged to someone else. How would I have felt if someone had given our confidential information to a competitor?

As I think back on that moment, however, I realize I failed. Not because I didn't study a competitor's numbers. I failed the person who sent it to me. Along with the confidential information that belonged to someone else, he passed a value judgment on to me that he should have been able to make on his own. I clearly knew that studying that report was wrong. But I never explained to him why it was legally and morally wrong, and I never let him know what I did with it. He may still think that I studied their numbers.

I've had P&Ls of competitors given to me on two other occasions. The second time, one of our regional vice presidents came to me and said, "Don, look what I found: a stack of all their monthly and annual performance reports!"

"We can't read those," I explained. I called the president of the company, a tough competitor, told him I'd put it in the mail, and assured him that his company's papers would not be copied or read. He thanked me profusely. I felt like I had done much better than the first time. I explained to the regional vice president who found them why we couldn't look at them. But I still made a mistake. There was one other thing I could have done better. I could have had the regional vice president talk to the competitor himself.

The last time a competitor's confidential data came to me, I had the man who found it call the president of the company and send it back. I think that had much greater impact on the individual rather than just taking care of it myself. The lesson of doing the right thing was much stronger because he was the one who had to follow through with it.

A bottom line principle of business—and of life—is,

to do what is right, even when no one else is looking. If I had allowed my regional manager to circulate the P&Ls, I would have had no business expecting honesty from anyone who worked for me. Likewise, we ought to do the right thing even if others around us seem to be backwards.

It was Mahatma Gandhi who said, "An error does not become truth by reason of multiplied propagation, nor does truth become error because nobody sees it."

As leaders, it is our job to create an environment through our words and actions so that others have the motivation to do right as well.

During the financial crisis, many exposed common practices of predatory lending, underwriting loans as a form of bribery, and whistleblower intimidation. An entire industry, totally upside-down, rocked our nation and the global economy. In the aftermath, we, the public, placed new demands on our corporate leaders. Many emerged from the recession calling for greater transparency. I started to hear new philosophies like 'Return on Integrity'. It's clear that we are redefining success for the modern-day corporation. And it has a lot to do with ethics, integrity, and responsibility.

Here's the bottom line: We, as leaders, ought to model integrity every day. It starts with how we handle the dilemmas that may seem small. Your decisions and actions set the tone for the culture and reinforce the expectation of others.

So, what ethical dilemmas have you encountered at work? In your personal life? What has been your first response? Has your personal integrity been your foremost concern or an afterthought? Are there choices you have made that you regret? Is there anything you can do to rectify wrongs?

Most importantly: Have you made a commitment to build a culture of integrity, starting with yourself, even when no one else is looking?

O Lord, who may abide in Your tent?
Who may dwell on Your Holy Hill?
He who walks with integrity, and works righteousness,
and speaks truth in his heart.

PSALMS 15:1-2 NASB

SHARING A VISION

Dream lofty dreams, and as you dream, so shall you become. Your vision is the promise of what you shall one day be; your ideal is the prophecy of what you shall at last unveil.

—JAMES LANE ALLEN

One of the most powerful business stories of the last two decades was what happened with Apple when Steve Jobs returned to the company in 1997. My career was spent in mass-market retail. I don't claim to know all the nuances of the high tech world. But we don't have to dig very deep to know Jobs' vision for Apple products and services: simple and intuitive.

My grandkids and great grandkids can do more with a smart phone and computer than I can—and make it look a whole lot easier than I can. But for a guy with white hair, I can get around all right on my iPhone. It's just what Jobs promised: simple and intuitive.

One of the most impressive things about Jobs was his skill when it came to sharing the Apple vision both inside and outside the company. His short, heart-felt keynote addresses are still very popular on YouTube even after his death. You don't have to look very far to find a treasure trove of his calm, direct—but passionate-- commentaries. Watch just a few, then read a few of his interviews, and you will quickly discover that he was committed to sharing his vision. Why? He was wowed by the vision himself.

One of the interesting business case studies over the next decade will be to see if the senior leadership at Apple can continue to cast that vision in their words— and in their products.

When he looked into the future, Sam didn't see Walmart as the largest retailer, let alone the largest company, in the world—which is what it would become. He simply wanted to provide a better shopping experience for everyday people living in small towns. He wanted to improve their standard of living by providing quality goods at low prices in a pleasant shopping environment. He wanted to accomplish this with a team of people who would embrace this same vision, and who were pleasant, hardworking, and dedicated. Sam checked a person's smile before he checked their educational background when he made his hiring decisions! He strongly believed that if his team of associates felt like they were part of a family, it would make his vision a joy and a success. And ultimately, as a smart businessman, Sam realized that if the stores were successful, he could continue to grow the company and touch more customers with his vision.

People have ambitious dreams and grand ideas for the future all the time. The reason they don't all succeed like Sam did is that they can't all build the needed support and enthusiasm of others—investors, customers, their own employees—and maybe even themselves. Sam knew that people always related much better and on a much deeper level to something that is worthwhile, more so than to financial objectives. Sam adopted a simple business plan that was fueled by a belief that it would make the world a better place. Did he really believe his model could change the world of retail? Yes, he did—passionately. And that was one of the key reasons his team embraced the vision.

The customers validated Sam's vision, too. They continued to shop at Walmart, making the idea a reality and helping it to grow beyond anything anyone ever anticipated. Sam never wavered in his vision to provide service to small town America. The vision grew, but the fundamental premise never changed: improve the standard of living for everyday people by providing a wide assortment of quality goods at low prices.

I've been retired from Walmart for over a decade. It doesn't mean I've lost interest in the success of the company. I visit often and make myself available to do whatever might be of help. I can say with absolute certainty, whenever the vision of providing *a wide assortment of quality goods at everyday low prices* has wavered, the company has suffered. When we return to that simple vision, we flourish.

What's your vision for your life? Your family? Your company? Does it inspire others? Does it inspire you?

Does it inspire you enough to stick with it? Does it inspire you enough to make sure everyone you encounter knows what you are really about?

Sam's vision for Walmart would have never worked had it not first inspired him. Neither will yours or mine!

Where there is no vision, the people are unrestrained,

but happy is he who keeps the law.

PROVERBS 29:18 NASB

BUILDING TRUST

....

Trust is the emotional glue that binds
followers and leaders together.

—WARREN BENNIS

....

Trust is the foundation of all life's relationships. It is an essential ingredient in successful leadership. It is not something that we are entitled to, either. You have to earn it.

When an individual gets promoted or a new leader joins an organization, regardless of their reputation, they must prove themselves. Certainly they must prove that they are technically competent. But most of all, everyone is watching how that individual treats people.

Do they genuinely care about us? Do they demonstrate a measure of humility, or do they have a big ego?

Are they someone who listens to our opinions, or do they feel they have all the answers?

Is this a person of integrity? Can we really trust them?

The way a new leader acts early in his or her job will show what kind of person he or she is. During that time frame, everyone develops their own long-lasting perception. And those perceptions—hard to change—determine how they respond to the new leadership long into the future.

I've only worked for three companies in my career and, when I joined each one, I had to establish trust all over again. When I started with Walmart, I came in as an executive vice president. I know there were others in the organization who wondered why Sam went outside the company rather than promoting them. I felt like I was under a microscope. My co-workers and new direct reports watched everything I did for a long time, examining my every move. It took a while before I began to feel like people really trusted me, and it was only then that I could really accomplish everything that I was brought into the company to do. It didn't matter that Sam trusted me. The people I worked with had to develop their own trust in me. If I disappointed or failed them in that period of scrutiny, it wouldn't have worked. It was up to me to demonstrate who I really was; I had to be trustworthy. I had to earn their respect.

What would have happened if I had done something inappropriate? What if I had lied to any one of them? Or didn't keep a promise? Or mistreated someone? I would have damaged our trust. And once trust is broken, it takes a long time to heal—if it ever heals at all. Sadly, during my career, I saw several people—sharp, talented people—lose trust and never regain it.

It's sad to see someone who is widely trusted fall from grace. I know the late college football coach Joe Paterno is still warmly remembered by millions of Penn State fans. But there is no question his incredible legacy was severely tarnished by the saddening reports in his assistant coach's child abuse trial during which the Penn State Board of Trustees fired Paterno for a failure of leadership.

Maybe every professional bicyclist was blood doping too, but Lance Armstrong looked us in the eye and said he wasn't. Despite his incredible accomplishments in winning seven Tour de France races; in overcoming cancer; in creating a great charity; for many, his legacy will be that he cheated and lied about it.

Roger Clemens, Barry Bonds … the list is just too

long. I'm not even going to start on politicians. As a person of deep faith, I would have to say nothing hurts more than to see a spiritual giant do something that breaks trust. It hurts even more because so many people are hurt and damaged by such a fall from grace.

If you want to lead, never forget that the standards for you are set very high. People look up to you.

Trust is a precious commodity in all of our relationships. We can't afford to lose it by compromising on our values. People are watching and counting on us.

Obviously, none of us is perfect. So if you do stumble, rectify the situation immediately. Don't try to claim you were misunderstood. Don't blame others. Simply apologize and move on. The sooner the better.

Do people trust you? Have you earned their trust? Have you made things right when you were wrong?

Be trustworthy.

Many people claim to be loyal,
but it is hard to find a trustworthy person.

PROVERBS 20:6 NCV

ACTING DECISIVELY

Thinking is easy, acting is difficult. And to put one's thoughts into action is the most difficult thing in the world.

—JOHANN WOLFGANG VAN GOETHE

General George Patton paraphrased a proverb when he said: "A good plan executed violently now is better than a perfect plan executed next week."

I think he nails it on the head. Some of us are so bent on achieving perfection that we don't get anything done.

It is the same way in our walk of faith. One anonymous poet shows how we often miss at least one of those steps when we encounter someone in need.

I was hungry
and you formed a debate team
to debate the pros and cons
of world hunger relief.

I was imprisoned
and you crept away busily
hoping someone would
somehow find time to visit me.

I was poorly clothed
and in your mind you disapproved
of my lack of style.

I was sick
and you thanked God
for your good health.

I was homeless
and you preached
about the spiritual shelter of the church.

I was lonely
and you muttered a quick prayer
and left me alone.

You seem so content
so pleased with your Christianity
but I'm still hungry
and lonely and cold.

One of my favorite Bible stories is in Nehemiah. God gave him the job of leading the Jews back to their homeland and rebuilding the walls of Jerusalem after a seventy-year exile during which the city had fallen into neglect and ruin. A number of local political leaders didn't want to see the wanderers regain their home.

Perhaps the most powerful of the antagonists, a man named Sanballat, approached Nehemiah as he began reconstruction and suggested, "Let's meet together and pray."

Nehemiah's answer was classic. Your Bible may not say it quite this way, but my paraphrase is simple and to-the-point: "We've already prayed. It's time to roll up our sleeves and build the wall."

I'm all for thinking things through. I want to know the facts before making a huge decision. But I also know that many leaders hide behind the "need" for more information, another report, yet another meeting and discussion. They end up with the disease of paralysis by analysis.

One of the greatest things Sam Walton taught me is that a leader stays involved in his business and close to his people so that he can determine the best course of action without wasting time. At Walmart, we constantly monitored our progress, visited stores, and talked to associates to find out how the company was doing on the ground. We always had plenty of information, so we didn't need to hold three days' worth of meetings to figure out what to do next. We made plans for improvement quickly, and then executed those plans immediately. If we made a decision in a meeting on Friday, you could see it reflected in stores by Monday morning. Today's great leaders will make sure they have all the important information, appropriate discussion, and reflection so that they can act decisively when time is of great importance.

Do you act decisively? Do you consistently find excuses to defer important decisions? Is it a lack of confidence? Are you too far removed from what works and doesn't work in your business? (Or family or church or community?) What can you do to make yourself more ready to act in a timely manner?

In the same way, faith by itself—that does nothing—is dead.

JAMES 2:17 NCV

SERVING OTHERS

....

Good leaders must first become good servants.

—ROBERT GREENLEAF

....

In his classic little novel, *Journey to the East*, Hermann Hesse spins a tale of a band of rich and powerful men who have been recruited for an adventure that promises them great wealth and glory. None of the men know the name of the mysterious man sponsoring the expedition, nor even the final destination of their journey. Their only information comes through a humble servant, Leo, who prepares their food, polishes their boots, and plays the guitar and sings to them each night as they fall to sleep.

After a time, the journey grows unpleasant and increasingly difficult as these powerful men jockey for position and bicker among themselves as to who should be the leader and make decisions. And when their servant Leo disappears one night, things take an even more dramatic turn for the worse. One by one, the men desert the party and return home, having been broken by this grand failure. One man determines that he will find the mysterious sponsor of the scheme to find out where they went wrong. It takes him years, but he finally tracks this shadowy character down, only to discover that it was Leo. Leo points out that as long as the group had a servant, they had a leader; when they lost their servant, they lost their leader.

Leo reminds the man what he already knew in his heart: Great tasks require great servants.

Do leaders today really serve? Lots of references to "servant leadership" fly around corporate discussions. But my observation is that few people really seem to understand or practice service. I see plenty of top leaders who seem much more interested in their own compensation, comfort, and welfare than they are about their associates, their product, and their customers.

Bill George, former CEO of Medtronic, has said, "We need authentic leaders who are committed to stewardship of their assets and to making a difference in the lives of the people they serve." Notice my added emphasis on 'serve.'

Jesus Christ, the greatest leader we could ever have, lived out servant leadership in every aspect of His life. He ministered to the poor (Luke 4:18). He gave up all the comforts of divinity to do the will of His Father, God (Matthew 8:20). He committed Himself to an unjust execution—one suited for a criminal—to reconcile our world to God, Who tolerates no sin (John 10:15).

In a May, 2013 Forbes article, James Heskett tells a simple story. He was attending a ServiceMaster board meeting in the nineties. Before the meeting started, CEO William Pollard spilled his coffee. There were quite a few volunteers to find someone from the janitorial staff to get things cleaned up. Heskett writes:

He proceeded to get down on his hands and knees to clean up the spill himself. The remarkable thing was that board members and employees alike hardly noticed as he did it. It was as if it was expected in a company with self-proclaimed servant leadership.

Bill Gates is still best known for building Microsoft and

making the office environment a more productive place. But perhaps in the future—twenty, fifty, a hundred years from now—he will be better known for his philanthropic giving and service. He and his wife Melinda have pledged $35 billion for various medical and educational causes worldwide.

He described what led him to pour his heart into this endeavor in a commencement speech he gave at Harvard in 2007.

> *If you believe that every life has equal value, it's revolting to learn that some lives are seen as worth saving and others are not. We said to ourselves: "This can't be true. But if it is true, it deserves to be the priority of our giving." So we began our work in the same way anyone here would begin it. We asked: "How could the world let these children die?"*

In the Great Room at Greystone, our executive retreat facility for The Soderquist Center, we have a beautiful bronze statue of Christ washing Peter's feet. It serves as a constant reminder to us of how we should lead: by lowering ourselves and serving others.

True servant leaders:

- Believe in and feel responsibility for the growth and development of their people.
- Share not only the responsibility but also the recognition for success with their people.
- Don't ask others to do what they aren't willing to do themselves. There are no tasks beneath them.
- Establish relationships built on mutual respect and trust—and not just among top executives but at every level of their companies.
- Care about and look for ways to meet the needs of everyone they come in contact with, including associates, suppliers, and customers.

How are you viewed at work? Egotistical? How about at home? Self-serving? Or, are those around you compelled to serve just as you serve them?

...The one who is the greatest among you must become like the youngest, and the leader like the servant.

LUKE 22:26 NASB

OVERCOMING ADVERSITY

....

We shall draw from the heart of suffering itself
the means of inspiration and survival.

—WINSTON CHURCHILL

....

Each year Forbes magazine releases a list called America's Most Promising Companies, made up of privately held, high growth companies with under $250 million in revenue. Amazingly a third of the top hundred companies on the 2013 list were founded during the global financial crisis of 2007—2008.

In an interview with CNNMoney (January 22, 2009), Jim Collins, author of *Good to Great*, commented on how great companies turned that same global financial crisis into opportunity:

> *In times of great duress, tumult, and uncertainty, you have*
> *to have moorings. Companies like P&G, GE, J&J, and*

IBM had an incredible fabric of values, of underlying ideals or principles that explained why it was important that they existed. One of the things that was very distinctive about P&G, for example, was that they said a customer will always be able to depend on the fact that a product is what we say it is – we will always build our reputation on quality. When they were under pressure to start cutting corners or use cheaper ingredients, they just didn't do that. What we have found is that what really matters is that you actually have core values – not what they are. The more challenged you are, the more you have to have your values. You need to preserve them consistently over time.

My friend, when you are most tempted to give up on your values—during times of extreme adversity—that's when you most need them as a leader, as a person.

I remember an acquaintance who was diagnosed with cancer at the age of sixty-four. Over the next thirteen months, he lost seventy pounds and endured treatments and surgeries—but came out cancer free. How'd he handle it? He bought a bike. He declared himself a "Lance

Armstrong wannabe" and determined that if Lance Armstrong could beat cancer and win the Tour de France, he could achieve great things after his cancer recovery, too. We may not respect Armstrong's accomplishments—now redacted—in the Tour after the uncovering of his doping scandals, but we can't discredit his rebound from cancer. Following that example, he became stronger and healthier than he was before his cancer diagnosis.

We can live, learn, and lead to the best of our abilities, with the highest standards of integrity and still get knocked flat on our faces. Our best plans, intentions, and prayers don't ensure a trouble-free life.

I might even go so far as to say that all great accomplishments will be accompanied by pain.

Privately, personally we may wonder: Does God hurt us in order to make us stronger? The Bible says that God doesn't tempt us (James 1:13). And He does not allow trials greater than we can handle to enter into our lives (1 Corinthians 10:13). The Bible also says we should "hold on" during our sufferings "because they are like a father's discipline" (Hebrews 12:7). The writer of the book of

Hebrews also calls for his persecuted flock of Christians not to "get tired and stop trying" (12:3). He reminds them that in tough times, if we want to win the race, we must get rid of things that hinder us and the sin that entangles us—we can't run with extra weight and with our shoelaces tied together. But even more importantly, the writer of Hebrews calls all of us to keep our eyes on Jesus, the author and perfecter of our faith, who showed us how to run the race of life with perseverance (12:4). When we see our final destination and know that others have gone before us, it makes even the difficult moments of the journey passable.

Here are a few reminders to bolster your soul when you experience pain in your life:

- God will not allow anything to happen to you that you cannot bear (1 Corinthians 10:13).
- God is able to transform painful experiences into profound and powerful life lessons (Romans 8:28).
- God uses those who have experienced pain to bring comfort to others who are hurting today (2 Corinthians 1:4).

God wants only what's best for us—but He knows that sometimes the only road to character is through pain. The good news is that Jesus runs beside us each step of the way.

What adversity are you facing in your business right now? In your personal life?

When you feel like you don't have a prayer, it is precisely the time to pray!

My brethren, count it all joy when you fall into various trials, knowing that the testing of your faith produces patience. But let patience have its perfect work, that you may be perfect and complete, lacking nothing.

JAMES 1:2-4 NKJV

LEAD TO MAKE A DIFFERENCE BY…

TRUSTING GOD

Walk boldly and wisely.
There is a hand above that will help you on.

—PHILIP JAMES BAILEY

I joined Walmart in April 1980. At that time, the company's annual sales were $1.2 billion. When I retired from the Board of Directors twenty-three years later, the company's sales were $244 billion that year, and we had become the largest company in the world. What an adventure!

I went to work for Walmart after having served as the president of Ben Franklin Stores and I already had strong feelings of awe and humility about where my career had taken me. I didn't enter the work world with any plans for carving out a huge business career for myself. Sure, I was ambitious and wanted to do well, but matters of faith and family were more important to me. That's how I'd been raised.

I've penned this book not from the perspective of a powerful mover and shaker who has all the answers—because I don't—but as someone who holds the simple belief that if you live your life in the right way guided by values, God will take care of the rest. God's plans will always be better than the ones we come up with ourselves. I'm a living testament to that!

I've made my share of mistakes along the way, and I know for a fact that it wasn't my wisdom and business skills that brought me success. I'm a blessed man. And one of my great blessings was working side by side with Sam Walton. He truly knew how to live, learn, and lead. He was generous to pass on what he believed and what he knew to thousands of others. I wrote this book hoping that as you read these short reflections from my personal life and thoughts, my relationship with Sam and other cherished colleagues, and my career at Walmart, you would be inspired to live, learn, and lead to your fullest.

You know by now that success can't come by reading a book or following a list of principles, no matter how wise and good they might be. Sure, those things may help and provide a nudge in the right direction, but what really matters most is your relationship with God. If you hear and heed nothing else in this book, what I hope and pray you take with you is a renewed sense of trust in the plans and purposes our loving God has for your life. With Him, you will have everything you need to best live, learn, and lead.

Trust in the Lord with all your heart,
and lean not on your own understanding; in all your ways
acknowledge Him, and He shall direct your paths.

PROVERBS 3:5-6 NKJV

PRAYER FOR LIVING

Dear Heavenly Father,

Thank You that You meet me where I am today. You know my needs. You care about me. You are good and kind.

Lord, help me live according to Your purposes. Create in me a clean heart, O God. May my day-to-day actions and interactions reflect You. Protect me from temptation. Help me to bless those around me.

Lord, make me willing and able to learn every day. Show me the truths You want me to know. Give me the humility to correct mistakes and realign my thinking according to Your Word.

Lord, I'm in awe of the responsibility I have to lead—and to follow—other people. Help me shepherd the people in my care with patience, love, and wisdom. Help me to follow the leaders in my life with loyalty and insight. Strengthen me, Lord God, and guide my every decision.

In Jesus' name I pray, Amen.

DEDICATION

I would like to dedicate this book to my family. In many respects they have traveled this journey with me. They have seen the good and the bad and have continued to love me and support me no matter what.

My wife, Jo, is a big reason our children have become the successful men and women they are today. She has always been there for each one of us and continues to be. She has always supported my decisions and together we are committed to impacting the lives of others.

I am very proud of the choices our children have made in their lives. Each one of them is a dedicated Christian, as are their spouses, and has chosen a field where they too are involved in impacting lives. Nothing could make me happier.

Mark, after a number of years on the mission field in the Indian subcontinent, moved back to the city of Chicago and has dedicated his life to serving The Lord in inner cities. After establishing ministries in numerous cities in the country he now serves as an elder and co-pastor of his inner city church.

Wendy played an instrumental role in the establishment of The Soderquist Center at John Brown University and has dedicated her energies, wisdom and commitment to excellence since our founding. She continues as the key thought leader in her senior leadership role at the Center where we strive to reach leaders with the transforming power of value-based leadership.

Sandie, after serving as a special-education elementary school teacher, led in the establishment of the women' ministry at our church and today is a mentor to many young women who are facing key issues and choices in their lives. She is sought after by many who admire her because of her passion for the way she lives her life.

Jeff chose the field of athletics and is the head women's basketball coach at John Brown University. He is dedicated to more than just winning basketball games but, more importantly, to demonstrating that what is learned on the court can be translated directly into living a productive and successful Christian life.

We raised our children to be independent thinkers and they have been instrumental in sharing their learning's and wisdom with their parents in a constructive and candid manner. They have helped to make me a better person as I *Live Learn and Lead*.

Our ten grandchildren are an absolute delight and help to keep us young in spirit. We are proud of who they are today and who they are becoming.

ABOUT THE AUTHOR

Don served over twenty years in leadership at Walmart. In 1988, Sam Walton appointed David Glass CEO and Don Soderquist COO. Under their watch, Walmart grew from annual sales of $16 billion in 1988 to over $244 billion in 2003, earning a place in history as the world's largest company.

Walmart's success is grounded in values of high ethical standards, a performance focus, and servant leadership philosophies. The company worked tirelessly to instill those values in the hearts of every associate. Don's passion now is to teach those same principles to companies and organizations around the world.

Don is Founding Executive of The Soderquist Center for Leadership and Ethics, providing direction and inspiration for the team. He is also the namesake of the John Brown University College of Business.

Visit www.soderquist.org for more information about The Soderquist Center for Leadership and Ethics and to purchase Don's books, *Live Learn Lead* and *The Walmart Way*, an inside perspective and first-hand account of the keys to Walmart's success.